Ivan Kushnir

Economy of Brazil

Series "Economy in countries"

first published: 2019
last updated: 2021-01-26

Ivan Kushnir. Economy of Brazil. Series "Economy in countries". - 2019. - 71 pages.

This book about the economy of Brazil from the 1970s to the 2010s. Source data from UN Data.

Size. In the 2010s, the GDP of Brazil was equal to $2.2 trillion per year; the value of agriculture was $95.1 billion; the value of industry was $334.5 billion. Since the share in the world is between 1% and 10%, the country is classified as a regional leader.

Productivity. In the 2010s, the GDP per capita was $10 619.0, the value of agriculture per capita was $467.2, the value of industry per capita was $1 643.4. Since the productivity is between the average and the average of above average, the economy is classified as developed.

Growth. In the 2010s, the growth of gross domestic product was 1.3%; the growth of agriculture was 3.4%; the growth of industry was 0.27%.

Structure. In the 2010s, the economy of Brazil included: services (47.5%), industry (18.1%), trade (15.5%), transportation (7.9%), construction (5.8%), and agriculture (5.1%).

Exports and imports. In the 2010s, the imports were 7.4% higher than the exports, the net imports were equal to 0.91% of the GDP. The technological structure of exports are not better than the structure of imports.

Consumption and reproduction. The attitude of reproduction to the consumption is not better than the global average, so the share of GDP in the world will not increase.

Series "Economy in countries": parallel.page.link/en

© Ivan Kushnir, 2019

All rights reserved.

ISBN: 9781794662056

Contents

Part I. Size	4
Chapter I. Gross domestic product	5
Chapter II. Value added	9
Chapter III. Gross national income	13
Part II. Structure	17
Chapter IV. Agriculture	18
Chapter V. Industry	22
Chapter 5.1. Manufacturing	26
Chapter VI. Construction	30
Chapter VII. Transportation	34
Chapter VIII. Trade	38
Chapter IX. Services	42
Part III. External relations	46
Chapter X. Exports	47
Chapter XI. Imports	51
Part IV. Consumption	55
Chapter XII. Government consumption expenditure	56
Chapter XIII. Household consumption expenditure	60
Chapter XIV. Food consumption	64
Part V. Reproduction	67
Chapter XV. Gross fixed capital formation	68

Part I. Size

	The 2010s
GDP	$2.2 trillion
The share in the world	2.8%
Share in the Americas	8.5%
Share in South America	53.6%

Chapter I. Gross domestic product

The Brazil's gross domestic product grew from $102.8 billion per year in the 1970s to $2.2 trillion per year in the 2010s, that is by $2.1 trillion or 21.0 times. The change occurred at $1.8 trillion due to a 6.4-fold increase in prices, as also at $140.5 billion due to a 1.7-fold increase in productivity, as well as at $94.3 billion due to the expansion in population. The average annual growth in gross domestic product is 3.4%. The minimum value of gross domestic product was in 1970 at $35.2 billion. The maximum value of GDP was in 2011 at $2.6 trillion.

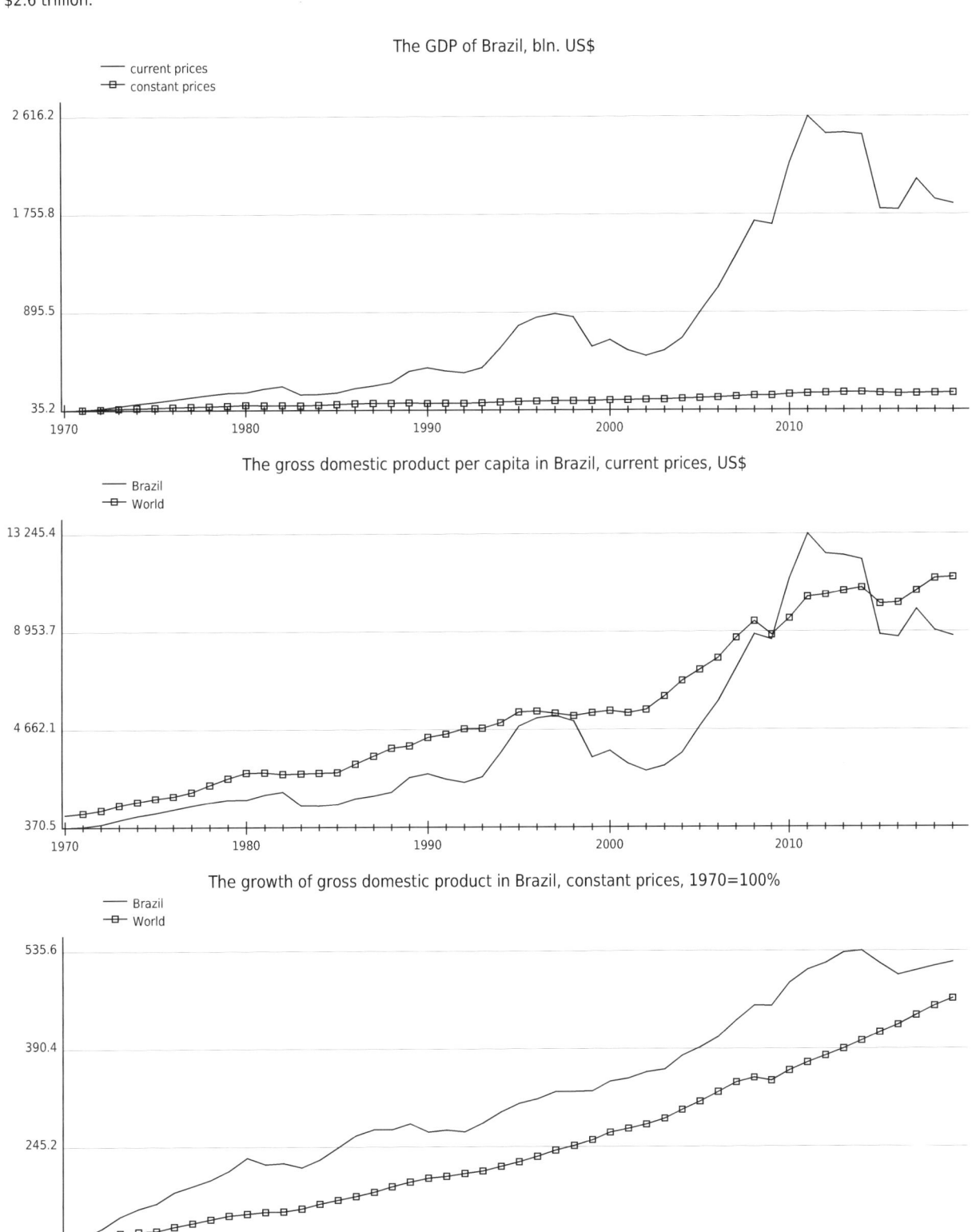

The 1970s

The Brazil's GDP was $102.8 billion per year in the 1970s, ranked 11th in the world. The share in the world was 1.6%, and 4.5% in the Americas.

The gross domestic product of Brazil consisted of: household consumption expenditure (69.1%), capital formation (23.0%), and public expenditure (10.0%).

The Brazil's GDP per capita was $968.3 in the 1970s, ranked 87th in the world, and was on a par with Anguilla ($969.1), Saint Kitts and Nevis ($953.2), Western Africa ($949.9). The Brazil's GDP per capita was less than gross domestic product per capita in the world ($1 620.8) by 40.3%, and was less than gross domestic product per capita in the Americas ($4 044.6) in 4.2 times.

The growth of gross domestic product in Brazil was 8.6% in the 1970s, ranked 20th in the world, and was on a par with Paraguay (8.5%), Singapore (8.6%). The growth of GDP in Brazil (8.6%) was greater than growth of gross domestic product in the world (4.1%), was greater than growth of gross domestic product in the Americas (4.1%).

Comparison with neighbors. The Brazil's gross domestic product was greater than in Argentina ($51.0 billion), in Venezuela ($31.0 billion), in Colombia ($20.4 billion), in Peru ($9.9 billion), in Uruguay ($4.1 billion), in Bolivia ($2.1 billion), and in Paraguay ($1.8 billion). The GDP per capita in Brazil was greater than in Colombia ($856.7), in Peru ($647.1), in Paraguay ($645.9), and in Bolivia ($424.4); but less than in Venezuela ($2.4 thousand), in Argentina ($1 988.4), and in Uruguay ($1 440.1). The growth of gross domestic product in Brazil was greater than in Paraguay (8.5%), in Colombia (5.7%), in Venezuela (4.8%), in Bolivia (4.5%), in Peru (3.4%), in Uruguay (2.7%), and in Argentina (2.7%).

Comparison with leaders. The GDP of Brazil was less than in the USA ($1.7 trillion), in the USSR ($649.4 billion), in Japan ($558.0 billion), in Germany ($484.2 billion), and in France ($333.2 billion). The gross domestic product per capita in Brazil was less than in the United States ($7.8 thousand), in France ($6.2 thousand), in Germany ($6.1 thousand), in Japan ($5.0 thousand), and in the USSR ($2.6 thousand). The growth of GDP in Brazil was greater than in the USSR (4.8%), in Japan (4.6%), in France (3.9%), in the United States (3.5%), and in Germany (3.1%).

The 1980s

The GDP of Brazil was $231.8 billion per year in the 1980s, ranked 12th in the world. The share in the world was 1.5%, and 4.3% in the Americas.

The GDP of Brazil consisted of: household expenditure (65.5%), capital formation (21.3%), government expenditure (11.2%), and net export (2.7%).

The gross domestic product per capita in Brazil was $1 733.7 in the 1980s, ranked 91st in the world, and was on a par with Fiji ($1 718.2), Colombia ($1 755.5). The Brazil's GDP per capita was less than gross domestic product per capita in the world ($3 123.4) by 44.5%, and was less than gross domestic product per capita in the Americas ($8 168.9) in 4.7 times.

The growth of GDP in Brazil was 2.9% in the 1980s, ranked 90th in the world, and was on a par with Eastern Africa (2.9%), Guinea (2.9%), Lesotho (2.9%). The growth of GDP in Brazil (2.9%) was less than growth of gross domestic product in the world (3.0%), was greater than growth of GDP in the Americas (2.8%).

Comparison with neighbors. The Brazil's GDP was greater than in Argentina ($99.6 billion), in Venezuela ($62.8 billion), in Colombia ($52.1 billion), in Peru ($22.8 billion), in Uruguay ($8.0 billion), in Paraguay ($6.0 billion), and in Bolivia ($4.1 billion). The gross domestic product per capita in Brazil was greater than in Paraguay ($1 657.1), in Peru ($1 164.4), and in Bolivia ($671.5); but less than in Venezuela ($3.7 thousand), in Argentina ($3.3 thousand), in Uruguay ($2.7 thousand), and in Colombia ($1 755.5). The growth of GDP in Brazil was greater than in Uruguay (0.96%), in Peru (0.078%), in Venezuela (-0.21%), in Bolivia (-0.44%), and in Argentina (-0.83%); but less than in Paraguay (3.9%) and in Colombia (3.4%).

Comparison with leaders. The GDP of Brazil was less than in the USA ($4.2 trillion), in Japan ($1.8 trillion), in Germany ($990.0 billion), in the USSR ($887.0 billion), and in France ($729.5 billion). The Brazil's GDP per capita was less than in the USA ($17.4 thousand), in Japan ($15.0 thousand), in France ($12.9 thousand), in Germany ($12.7 thousand), and in the USSR ($3.2 thousand). The growth of GDP in Brazil was greater than in France (2.3%) and in Germany (1.9%); but less than in the USSR (4.3%), in Japan (4.3%), and in the United States (3.1%).

The 1990s

Chapter I. Gross domestic product

The Brazilian gross domestic product was $609.3 billion per year in the 1990s, ranked 9th in the world, and was on a par with Canada ($616.6 billion), Southern Asia ($601.6 billion). The share in the world was 2.1%, and 6.1% in the Americas.

The GDP of Brazil included: household expenditure (63.6%), public expenditure (19.3%), and capital formation (18.5%).

The Brazil's GDP per capita was $3 790.9 in the 1990s, ranked 74th in the world, and was on a par with Dominica ($3.8 thousand), South America ($3.8 thousand). The Brazil's GDP per capita was less than GDP per capita in the world ($5 020.1) by 24.5%, and was less than gross domestic product per capita in the Americas ($12 984.7) in 3.4 times.

The growth of gross domestic product in Brazil was 1.6% in the 1990s, ranked 148th in the world, and was on a par with Togo (1.6%). The growth of GDP in Brazil (1.6%) was less than growth of GDP in the world (2.8%), was less than growth of gross domestic product in the Americas (3.1%).

Comparison with neighbors. The GDP of Brazil was greater than in Argentina ($266.6 billion), in Colombia ($91.3 billion), in Venezuela ($69.1 billion), in Peru ($45.1 billion), in Uruguay ($18.8 billion), in Paraguay ($9.0 billion), and in Bolivia ($6.6 billion). The GDP per capita in Brazil was greater than in Venezuela ($3.2 thousand), in Colombia ($2.5 thousand), in Paraguay ($1 913.6), in Peru ($1 873.3), and in Bolivia ($879.3); but less than in Argentina ($7.7 thousand) and in Uruguay ($5.8 thousand). The growth of gross domestic product in Brazil was less than in Argentina (4.2%), in Bolivia (4.0%), in Uruguay (3.4%), in Peru (3.1%), in Colombia (2.8%), in Venezuela (2.4%), and in Paraguay (2.2%).

Comparison with leaders. The Brazilian GDP was less than in the USA ($7.6 trillion), in Japan ($4.3 trillion), in Germany ($2.2 trillion), in France ($1.4 trillion), and in the United Kingdom ($1.3 trillion). The gross domestic product per capita in Brazil was less than in Japan ($34.3 thousand), in the United States ($28.7 thousand), in Germany ($27.0 thousand), in France ($24.1 thousand), and in the UK ($22.9 thousand). The growth of GDP in Brazil was greater than in Japan (1.5%); but less than in the United States (3.2%), in the UK (2.3%), in Germany (2.2%), and in France (2.0%).

The 2000s

The GDP of Brazil was $971.3 billion per year in the 2000s, ranked 10th in the world, and was on a par with Central America ($963.8 billion). The share in the world was 2.1%, and 5.8% in the Americas.

The GDP of Brazil included: household expenditure (61.0%), government consumption expenditure (19.1%), and capital formation (19.1%).

The GDP per capita in Brazil was $5 256.7 in the 2000s, ranked 87th in the world, and was on a par with Panama ($5.2 thousand). The gross domestic product per capita in Brazil was less than GDP per capita in the world ($7 176.3) by 26.7%, and was less than gross domestic product per capita in the Americas ($19 020.5) in 3.6 times.

The growth of GDP in Brazil was 3.3% in the 2000s, ranked 125th in the world, and was on a par with South America (3.3%). The growth of gross domestic product in Brazil (3.3%) was greater than growth of gross domestic product in the world (3.0%), was greater than growth of GDP in the Americas (2.1%).

Comparison with neighbors. The Brazil's gross domestic product was greater than in Argentina ($244.3 billion), in Venezuela ($173.3 billion), in Colombia ($149.2 billion), in Peru ($79.3 billion), in Uruguay ($20.5 billion), in Paraguay ($13.5 billion), and in Bolivia ($10.9 billion). The gross domestic product per capita in Brazil was greater than in Colombia ($3.5 thousand), in Peru ($2.9 thousand), in Paraguay ($2.3 thousand), and in Bolivia ($1 196.1); but less than in Venezuela ($6.6 thousand), in Argentina ($6.3 thousand), and in Uruguay ($6.2 thousand). The growth of gross domestic product in Brazil was greater than in Argentina (2.3%) and in Uruguay (2.1%); but less than in Peru (5.0%), in Paraguay (4.0%), in Colombia (3.9%), in Bolivia (3.7%), and in Venezuela (3.7%).

Comparison with leaders. The Brazil's GDP was less than in the USA ($12.6 trillion), in Japan ($4.7 trillion), in Germany ($2.8 trillion), in China ($2.6 trillion), and in the UK ($2.3 trillion). The GDP per capita in Brazil was greater than in China ($1 954.1); but less than in the United States ($42.8 thousand), in the UK ($38.4 thousand), in Japan ($36.4 thousand), and in Germany ($34.0 thousand). The growth of gross domestic product in Brazil was greater than in the United States (1.9%), in the UK (1.7%), in Germany (0.73%), and in Japan (0.50%); but less than in China (10.3%).

The 2010s

The Brazilian gross domestic product was $2.2 trillion per year in the 2010s, ranked 8th in the world, and was on a par with India ($2.2 trillion). The share in the world was 2.8%, and 8.5% in the Americas.

The gross domestic product of Brazil included: household expenditure (62.7%), government consumption expenditure (19.4%), and capital formation (18.8%).

The Brazil's gross domestic product per capita was $10 619.0 in the 2010s, ranked 82nd in the world, and was on a par with the World ($10.6 thousand), Kazakhstan ($10.7 thousand), Malaysia ($10.6 thousand). The GDP per capita in Brazil was greater than gross domestic product per capita in the world ($10 603.1) by 0.15%, and was less than GDP per capita in the Americas ($26 129.9) in 2.5 times.

The growth of GDP in Brazil was 1.3% in the 2010s, ranked 170th in the world. The growth of gross domestic product in Brazil (1.3%) was less than growth of gross domestic product in the world (3.1%), was less than growth of gross domestic product in the Americas (2.2%).

Comparison with neighbors. The GDP of Brazil was 3.9 times higher than in Argentina ($553.3 billion), 6.5 times higher than in Colombia ($330.1 billion), 7.1 times higher than in Venezuela ($304.6 billion), 11.1 times higher than in Peru ($195.6 billion), 40.4 times higher than in Uruguay ($53.5 billion), 59.6 times higher than in Paraguay ($36.3 billion), and 67.5 times higher than in Bolivia ($32.0 billion). The gross domestic product per capita in Brazil was 2.2% higher than in Venezuela ($10.4 thousand), 52.8% higher than in Colombia ($6.9 thousand), 65.6% higher than in Peru ($6.4 thousand), 94.5% higher than in Paraguay ($5.5 thousand), and 3.6 times higher than in Bolivia ($3.0 thousand); but 32.4% lower than in Uruguay ($15.7 thousand) and 17.8% lower than in Argentina ($12.9 thousand). The growth of gross domestic product in Brazil was greater than in Argentina (1.3%) and in Venezuela (-9.7%); but less than in Bolivia (4.6%), in Peru (4.5%), in Paraguay (4.4%), in Colombia (3.7%), and in Uruguay (3.1%).

Comparison with leaders. The Brazilian gross domestic product was 8.3 times lower than in the United States ($18.0 trillion), 4.9 times lower than in China ($10.5 trillion), 2.4 times lower than in Japan ($5.2 trillion), 41.0% lower than in Germany ($3.7 trillion), and 21.9% lower than in the UK ($2.8 trillion). The GDP per capita in Brazil was 41.8% higher than in China ($7.5 thousand); but 5.3 times lower than in the USA ($56.2 thousand), 4.2 times lower than in Germany ($44.7 thousand), 4.0 times lower than in the UK ($42.2 thousand), and 3.8 times lower than in Japan ($40.9 thousand). The growth of gross domestic product in Brazil was greater than in Japan (1.3%); but less than in China (7.7%), in the United States (2.3%), in Germany (1.9%), and in the United Kingdom (1.8%).

Chapter II. Value added

The Brazilian value added grew up from $97.5 billion per year in the 1970s to $1.8 trillion per year in the 2010s, that is by $1.8 trillion or 19.0 times. The change occurred at $1.5 trillion due to a 5.6-fold increase in prices, as also at $140.5 billion due to a 1.8-fold increase in productivity, as well as at $89.4 billion due to the growth in population. The average annual growth in value added is 3.5%. The minimum value of value added was in 1970 at $31.6 billion. The maximum value of value added was in 2011 at $2.2 trillion.

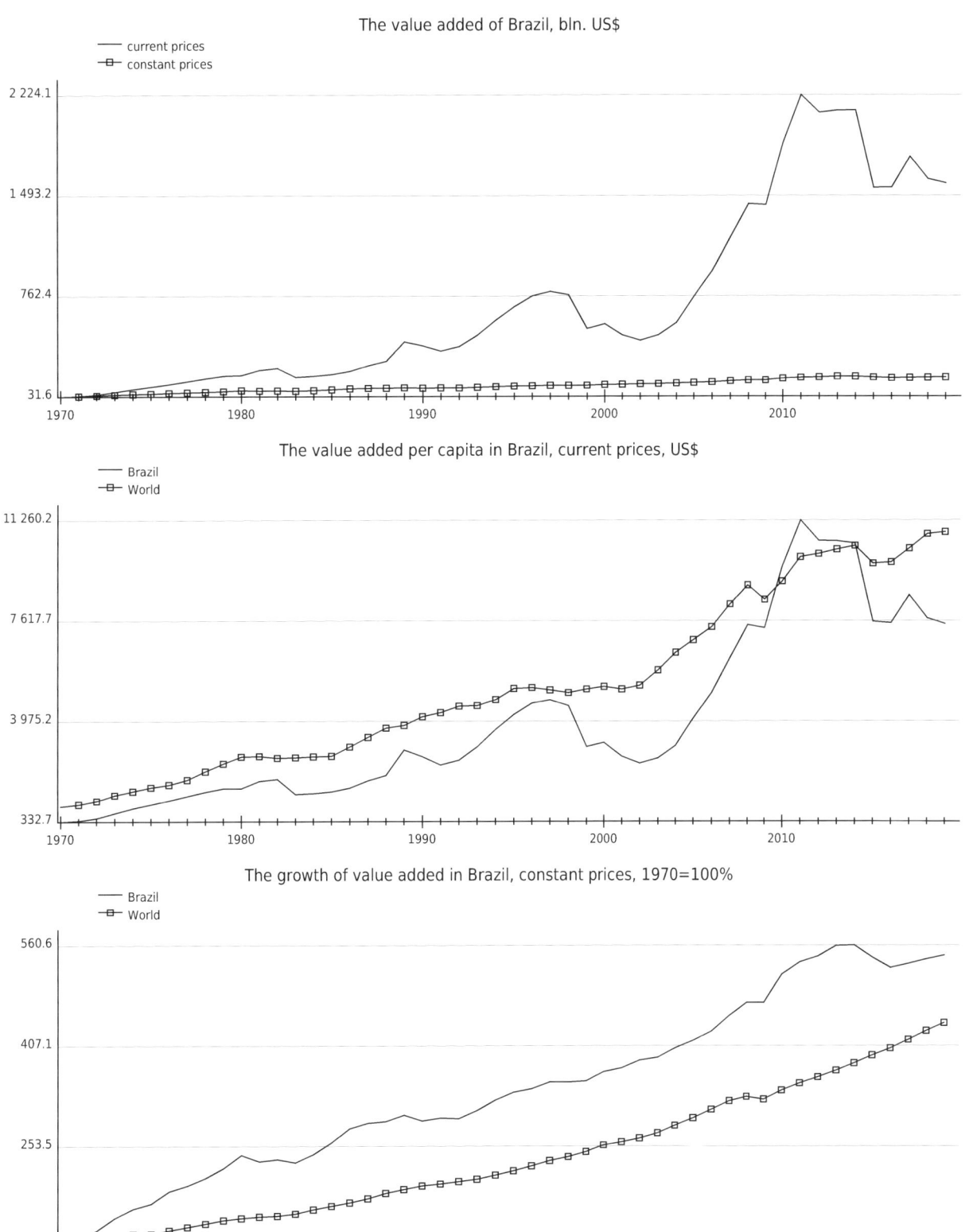

The 1970s

The Brazilian value added was $97.5 billion per year in the 1970s, ranked 12th in the world, and was on a par with Mexico ($99.1 billion). The share in the world was 1.5%, and 4.4% in the Americas.

The total value added of Brazil included: industry (33.1%), services (31.7%), trade (13.4%), agriculture (11.1%), construction (6.3%), and transportation (4.5%).

The value added per capita in Brazil was $918.5 in the 1970s, ranked 87th in the world, and was on a par with Western Africa ($914.0), Micronesia ($912.7), the Seychelles ($907.5). The value added per capita in Brazil was less than value added per capita in the world ($1 564.4) by 41.3%, and was less than value added per capita in the Americas ($3 985.3) in 4.3 times.

The growth of value added in Brazil was 9.2% in the 1970s, ranked 12th in the world, and was on a par with the Solomon Islands (9.1%), Aruba (9.1%). The growth of value added in Brazil (9.2%) was greater than growth of value added in the world (3.9%), was greater than growth of value added in the Americas (3.5%).

Comparison with neighbors. The value added of Brazil was greater than in Argentina ($46.4 billion), in Venezuela ($31.5 billion), in Colombia ($19.9 billion), in Peru ($9.7 billion), in Uruguay ($3.6 billion), in Bolivia ($2.1 billion), and in Paraguay ($1.8 billion). The Brazilian value added per capita was greater than in Colombia ($833.2), in Paraguay ($660.7), in Peru ($636.6), and in Bolivia ($414.9); but less than in Venezuela ($2.4 thousand), in Argentina ($1 806.7), and in Uruguay ($1 261.4). The growth of value added in Brazil was greater than in Paraguay (8.2%), in Colombia (5.7%), in Bolivia (5.3%), in Venezuela (4.6%), in Peru (3.4%), in Uruguay (2.7%), and in Argentina (2.7%).

Comparison with leaders. The Brazilian value added was less than in the United States ($1.7 trillion), in the USSR ($649.4 billion), in Japan ($545.3 billion), in Germany ($444.9 billion), and in France ($297.3 billion). The Brazil's value added per capita was less than in the United States ($7.8 thousand), in Germany ($5.7 thousand), in France ($5.5 thousand), in Japan ($4.9 thousand), and in the USSR ($2.6 thousand). The growth of value added in Brazil was greater than in Japan (4.9%), in the USSR (4.8%), in France (3.7%), in Germany (3.1%), and in the USA (2.9%).

The 1980s

The Brazilian value added was $238.2 billion per year in the 1980s, ranked 10th in the world, and was on a par with Spain ($236.5 billion), Mexico ($235.4 billion), Oceania ($242.8 billion). The share in the world was 1.6%, and 4.4% in the Americas.

The total value added of Brazil consisted of: services (36.4%), industry (33.5%), agriculture (9.8%), trade (8.5%), construction (6.9%), and transportation (5.0%).

The Brazil's value added per capita was $1 782.1 in the 1980s, ranked 88th in the world, and was on a par with Ecuador ($1 793.2), Fiji ($1 797.8), Bulgaria ($1 799.5). The value added per capita in Brazil was less than value added per capita in the world ($3 029.9) by 41.2%, and was less than value added per capita in the Americas ($8 159.2) in 4.6 times.

The growth of value added in Brazil was 3.2% in the 1980s, ranked 77th in the world, and was on a par with Portugal (3.2%), Palau (3.2%), Jordan (3.2%). The growth of value added in Brazil (3.2%) was greater than growth of value added in the world (2.9%), was greater than growth of value added in the Americas (2.7%).

Comparison with neighbors. The value added of Brazil was greater than in Argentina ($91.8 billion), in Venezuela ($63.1 billion), in Colombia ($50.0 billion), in Peru ($23.1 billion), in Uruguay ($7.3 billion), in Paraguay ($6.3 billion), and in Bolivia ($4.0 billion). The Brazilian value added per capita was greater than in Paraguay ($1 737.7), in Colombia ($1 687.4), in Peru ($1 182.8), and in Bolivia ($655.6); but less than in Venezuela ($3.7 thousand), in Argentina ($3.1 thousand), and in Uruguay ($2.4 thousand). The growth of value added in Brazil was greater than in Uruguay (0.76%), in Peru (0.078%), in Venezuela (-0.40%), in Bolivia (-0.53%), and in Argentina (-0.63%); but less than in Colombia (3.7%) and in Paraguay (3.4%).

Comparison with leaders. The Brazil's value added was less than in the USA ($4.2 trillion), in Japan ($1.8 trillion), in Germany ($907.0 billion), in the USSR ($887.0 billion), and in France ($650.9 billion). The Brazilian value added per capita was less than in the USA ($17.4 thousand), in Japan ($14.8 thousand), in Germany ($11.6 thousand), in France ($11.5 thousand), and in the USSR ($3.2 thousand). The growth of value added in Brazil was greater than in the USA (2.8%), in France (2.2%), and in Germany (2.0%); but less than in the USSR (4.3%) and in Japan (4.2%).

The 1990s

Chapter II. Value added

The value added of Brazil was $575.8 billion per year in the 1990s, ranked 8th in the world, and was on a par with Canada ($571.5 billion), South-Eastern Asia ($570.7 billion), Africa ($561.8 billion). The share in the world was 2.1%, and 5.8% in the Americas.

The total value added of Brazil consisted of: services (52.1%), industry (22.2%), trade (9.1%), agriculture (6.4%), construction (6.1%), and transportation (4.1%).

The Brazil's value added per capita was $3 582.9 in the 1990s, ranked 74th in the world, and was on a par with Hungary ($3.6 thousand), Croatia ($3.5 thousand), Turkey ($3.6 thousand). The Brazilian value added per capita was less than value added per capita in the world ($4 799.9) by 25.4%, and was less than value added per capita in the Americas ($12 777.9) in 3.6 times.

The growth of value added in Brazil was 1.6% in the 1990s, ranked 146th in the world. The growth of value added in Brazil (1.6%) was less than growth of value added in the world (2.7%), was less than growth of value added in the Americas (2.8%).

Comparison with neighbors. The Brazil's value added was greater than in Argentina ($236.1 billion), in Colombia ($87.2 billion), in Venezuela ($66.9 billion), in Peru ($41.2 billion), in Uruguay ($17.4 billion), in Paraguay ($9.1 billion), and in Bolivia ($6.1 billion). The value added per capita in Brazil was greater than in Venezuela ($3.1 thousand), in Colombia ($2.4 thousand), in Paraguay ($1 930.1), in Peru ($1 709.6), and in Bolivia ($804.4); but less than in Argentina ($6.8 thousand) and in Uruguay ($5.4 thousand). The growth of value added in Brazil was less than in Argentina (4.3%), in Bolivia (4.3%), in Peru (3.1%), in Uruguay (2.8%), in Colombia (2.6%), in Paraguay (2.0%), and in Venezuela (2.0%).

Comparison with leaders. The Brazilian value added was less than in the United States ($7.6 trillion), in Japan ($4.3 trillion), in Germany ($2.0 trillion), in France ($1.3 trillion), and in the United Kingdom ($1.2 trillion). The value added per capita in Brazil was less than in Japan ($34.2 thousand), in the USA ($28.6 thousand), in Germany ($24.5 thousand), in France ($21.6 thousand), and in the UK ($21.4 thousand). The growth of value added in Brazil was less than in the USA (2.8%), in the United Kingdom (2.4%), in Germany (2.1%), in France (1.8%), and in Japan (1.8%).

The 2000s

The Brazil's value added was $827.1 billion per year in the 2000s, ranked 11th in the world, and was on a par with Mexico ($830.3 billion). The share in the world was 1.9%, and 5.1% in the Americas.

The total value added of Brazil included: services (46.8%), industry (22.2%), trade (12.9%), transportation (7.6%), agriculture (5.6%), and construction (4.8%).

The value added per capita in Brazil was $4 476.3 in the 2000s, ranked 90th in the world, and was on a par with Costa Rica ($4.5 thousand), Saint Vincent ($4.4 thousand). The value added per capita in Brazil was less than value added per capita in the world ($6 818.0) by 34.3%, and was less than value added per capita in the Americas ($18 623.4) in 4.2 times.

The growth of value added in Brazil was 3% in the 2000s, ranked 132nd in the world, and was on a par with Somalia (3.0%), Slovenia (3.0%), Oceania (3.0%). The growth of value added in Brazil (3.0%) was greater than growth of value added in the world (2.9%), was greater than growth of value added in the Americas (1.9%).

Comparison with neighbors. The value added of Brazil was greater than in Argentina ($209.4 billion), in Venezuela ($164.8 billion), in Colombia ($136.2 billion), in Peru ($72.5 billion), in Uruguay ($18.6 billion), in Paraguay ($13.1 billion), and in Bolivia ($9.3 billion). The value added per capita in Brazil was greater than in Colombia ($3.2 thousand), in Peru ($2.6 thousand), in Paraguay ($2.3 thousand), and in Bolivia ($1 021.4); but less than in Venezuela ($6.3 thousand), in Uruguay ($5.6 thousand), and in Argentina ($5.4 thousand). The growth of value added in Brazil was greater than in Argentina (2.2%) and in Uruguay (1.8%); but less than in Peru (4.1%), in Colombia (3.8%), in Venezuela (3.8%), in Bolivia (3.5%), and in Paraguay (3.0%).

Comparison with leaders. The Brazil's value added was less than in the United States ($12.6 trillion), in Japan ($4.7 trillion), in China ($2.6 trillion), in Germany ($2.5 trillion), and in the UK ($2.1 trillion). The value added per capita in Brazil was greater than in China ($1 954.1); but less than in the United States ($42.8 thousand), in Japan ($36.4 thousand), in the UK ($34.6 thousand), and in Germany ($30.7 thousand). The growth of value added in Brazil was greater than in the USA (1.7%), in the United Kingdom (1.7%), in Germany (0.65%), and in Japan (0.27%); but less than in China (10.2%).

The 2010s

The Brazilian value added was $1.8 trillion per year in the 2010s, ranked 8th in the world, and was on a par with Italy ($1.8 trillion). The share in the world was 2.5%, and 7.5% in the Americas.

The total value added of Brazil included: services (47.5%), industry (18.1%), trade (15.5%), transportation (7.9%), construction (5.8%), and agriculture (5.1%).

The Brazil's value added per capita was $9 088.1 in the 2010s, ranked 85th in the world. The value added per capita in Brazil was less than value added per capita in the world ($10 094.6) by 10.0%, and was less than value added per capita in the Americas ($25 411.8) in 2.8 times.

The growth of value added in Brazil was 1.4% in the 2010s, ranked 170th in the world, and was on a par with Samoa (1.4%), Lebanon (1.4%). The growth of value added in Brazil (1.4%) was less than growth of value added in the world (3.1%), was less than growth of value added in the Americas (2.1%).

Comparison with neighbors. The Brazil's value added was 4.0 times higher than in Argentina ($465.4 billion), 6.2 times higher than in Colombia ($300.3 billion), 6.5 times higher than in Venezuela ($286.1 billion), 10.3 times higher than in Peru ($179.2 billion), 38.1 times higher than in Uruguay ($48.5 billion), 55.0 times higher than in Paraguay ($33.6 billion), and 69.2 times higher than in Bolivia ($26.7 billion). The Brazilian value added per capita was 43.8% higher than in Colombia ($6.3 thousand), 54.7% higher than in Peru ($5.9 thousand), 79.6% higher than in Paraguay ($5.1 thousand), and 3.7 times higher than in Bolivia ($2.5 thousand); but 36.2% lower than in Uruguay ($14.2 thousand), 16.3% lower than in Argentina ($10.9 thousand), and 6.8% lower than in Venezuela ($9.8 thousand). The growth of value added in Brazil was greater than in Argentina (1.2%) and in Venezuela (-8.1%); but less than in Bolivia (4.6%), in Peru (4.4%), in Paraguay (4.2%), in Colombia (3.6%), and in Uruguay (3.0%).

Comparison with leaders. The Brazilian value added was 9.7 times lower than in the United States ($18.0 trillion), 5.7 times lower than in China ($10.5 trillion), 2.8 times lower than in Japan ($5.2 trillion), 44.0% lower than in Germany ($3.3 trillion), and 25.1% lower than in the UK ($2.5 trillion). The value added per capita in Brazil was 21.3% higher than in China ($7.5 thousand); but 6.2 times lower than in the United States ($56.2 thousand), 4.5 times lower than in Japan ($40.7 thousand), 4.4 times lower than in Germany ($40.3 thousand), and 4.1 times lower than in the United Kingdom ($37.7 thousand). The growth of value added in Brazil was greater than in Japan (1.3%); but less than in China (7.7%), in the United States (2.2%), in Germany (1.9%), and in the United Kingdom (1.8%).

Chapter III. Gross national income

The Brazilian gross national income increased from $101.1 billion per year in the 1970s to $2.1 trillion per year in the 2010s, that is by $2.0 trillion or 20.9 times. The change occurred at $1.8 trillion due to a 6.4-fold increase in prices, as also at $135.7 billion due to a 1.7-fold increase in productivity, as well as at $92.7 billion due to the growth in population. The average annual growth in gross national income is 3.4%. The minimum value of gross national income was in 1970 at $34.9 billion. The maximum value of gross national income was in 2011 at $2.5 trillion.

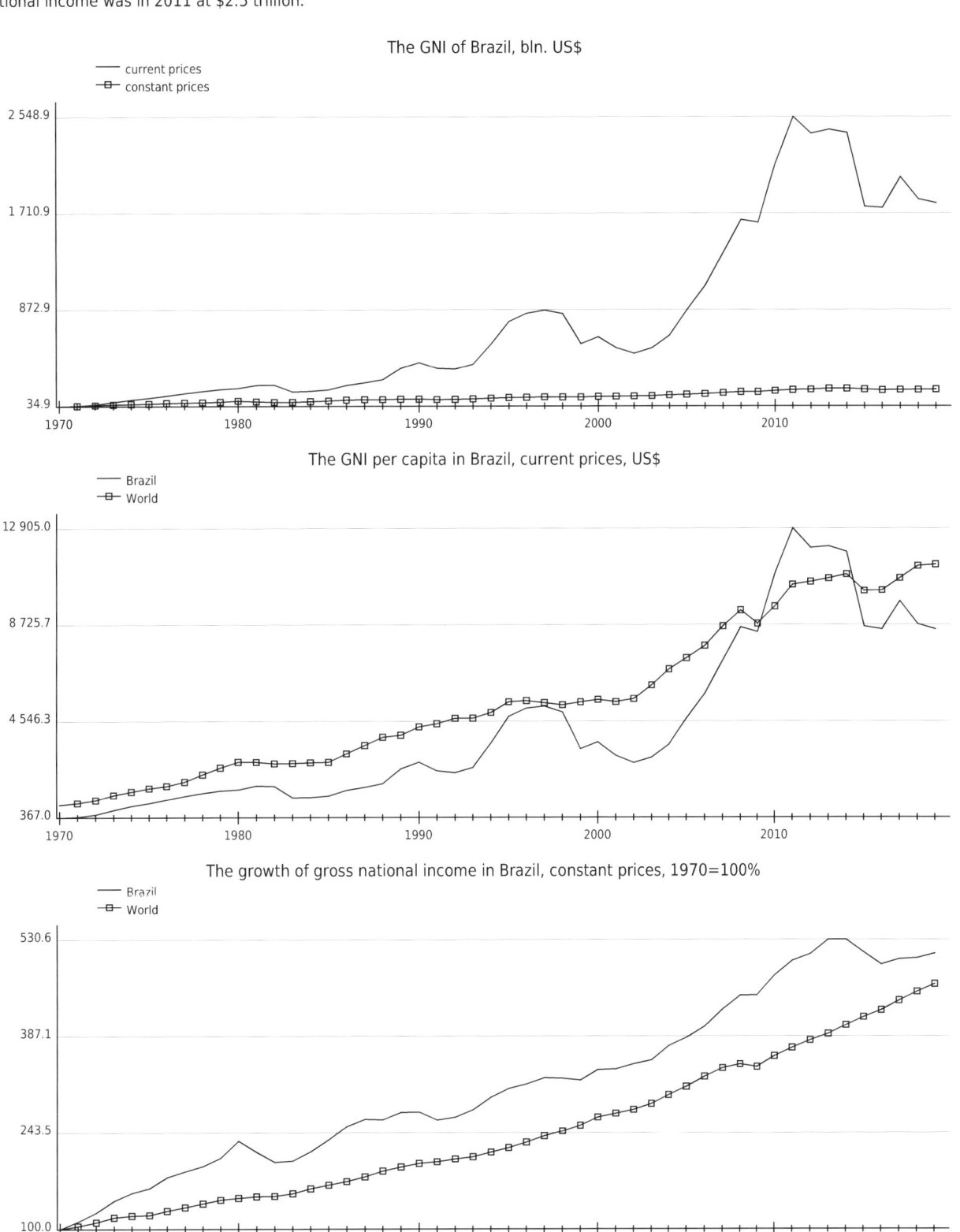

The 1970s

The gross national income of Brazil was $101.1 billion per year in the 1970s, ranked 11th in the world, and was on a par with India ($99.7 billion). The share in the world was 1.5%, and 4.5% in the Americas.

The GNI per capita in Brazil was $952.0 in the 1970s, ranked 87th in the world, and was on a par with Western Africa ($938.0), Fiji ($969.8). The gross national income per capita in Brazil was less than GNI per capita in the world ($1 624.3) by 41.4%, and was less than GNI per capita in the Americas ($4 019.9) in 4.2 times.

The growth of GNI in Brazil was 8.3% in the 1970s, ranked 24th in the world, and was on a par with the Seychelles (8.4%). The growth of gross national income in Brazil (8.3%) was greater than growth of GNI in the world (4.1%), was greater than growth of GNI in the Americas (4.0%).

Comparison with neighbors. The GNI of Brazil was greater than in Argentina ($50.1 billion), in Venezuela ($30.3 billion), in Colombia ($20.1 billion), in Peru ($9.6 billion), in Uruguay ($4.0 billion), in Bolivia ($2.1 billion), and in Paraguay ($1.6 billion). The gross national income per capita in Brazil was greater than in Colombia ($843.9), in Peru ($630.7), in Paraguay ($581.4), and in Bolivia ($419.7); but less than in Venezuela ($2.3 thousand), in Argentina ($1 953.3), and in Uruguay ($1 425.6). The growth of gross national income in Brazil was greater than in Colombia (5.9%), in Argentina (5.5%), in Venezuela (5.4%), in Bolivia (4.0%), in Peru (2.9%), and in Uruguay (2.7%); but less than in Paraguay (8.8%).

Comparison with leaders. The GNI of Brazil was less than in the USA ($1.7 trillion), in the USSR ($649.4 billion), in Japan ($558.5 billion), in Germany ($486.2 billion), and in France ($334.3 billion). The Brazil's GNI per capita was less than in the USA ($7.8 thousand), in France ($6.2 thousand), in Germany ($6.2 thousand), in Japan ($5.0 thousand), and in the USSR ($2.6 thousand). The growth of GNI in Brazil was greater than in the USSR (4.8%), in Japan (4.7%), in France (3.9%), in the USA (3.5%), and in Germany (3.0%).

The 1980s

The GNI of Brazil was $221.1 billion per year in the 1980s, ranked 12th in the world. The share in the world was 1.5%, and 4.1% in the Americas.

The gross national income per capita in Brazil was $1 654.2 in the 1980s, ranked 91st in the world, and was on a par with the Marshall Islands ($1 624.1), Fiji ($1 622.1). The Brazilian GNI per capita was less than GNI per capita in the world ($3 117.1) by 46.9%, and was less than gross national income per capita in the Americas ($8 063.2) in 4.9 times.

The growth of gross national income in Brazil was 2.9% in the 1980s, ranked 92nd in the world, and was on a par with Australasia (2.9%), Oceania (2.9%), Norway (2.9%). The growth of GNI in Brazil (2.9%) was less than growth of GNI in the world (3.0%), was greater than growth of gross national income in the Americas (2.8%).

Comparison with neighbors. The Brazil's GNI was greater than in Argentina ($94.9 billion), in Venezuela ($61.0 billion), in Colombia ($50.5 billion), in Peru ($22.1 billion), in Uruguay ($7.8 billion), in Paraguay ($5.4 billion), and in Bolivia ($3.9 billion). The GNI per capita in Brazil was greater than in Paraguay ($1 499.5), in Peru ($1 128.9), and in Bolivia ($629.9); but less than in Venezuela ($3.6 thousand), in Argentina ($3.2 thousand), in Uruguay ($2.6 thousand), and in Colombia ($1 701.6). The growth of GNI in Brazil was greater than in Uruguay (0.63%), in Peru (0.62%), in Venezuela (-0.51%), in Bolivia (-0.59%), and in Argentina (-1.6%); but less than in Paraguay (4.1%) and in Colombia (3.0%).

Comparison with leaders. The gross national income of Brazil was less than in the United States ($4.2 trillion), in Japan ($1.8 trillion), in Germany ($996.5 billion), in the USSR ($887.0 billion), and in France ($732.1 billion). The Brazil's GNI per capita was less than in the United States ($17.4 thousand), in Japan ($15.0 thousand), in France ($13.0 thousand), in Germany ($12.8 thousand), and in the USSR ($3.2 thousand). The growth of gross national income in Brazil was greater than in France (2.3%) and in Germany (2.0%); but less than in Japan (4.4%), in the USSR (4.3%), and in the USA (3.1%).

The 1990s

The Brazilian GNI was $600.0 billion per year in the 1990s, ranked 8th in the world, and was on a par with Southern Asia ($598.5 billion), Canada ($595.6 billion). The share in the world was 2.1%, and 6.1% in the Americas.

The GNI per capita in Brazil was $3 733.5 in the 1990s, ranked 73rd in the world, and was on a par with Dominica ($3.7 thousand), South America ($3.7 thousand), Central America ($3.7 thousand). The gross national income per capita in Brazil was less than GNI per

Chapter III. Gross national income

capita in the world ($4 991.4) by 25.2%, and was less than gross national income per capita in the Americas ($12 792.4) in 3.4 times.

The growth of gross national income in Brazil was 1.6% in the 1990s, ranked 147th in the world. The growth of gross national income in Brazil (1.6%) was less than growth of GNI in the world (2.8%), was less than growth of GNI in the Americas (3.2%).

Comparison with neighbors. The gross national income of Brazil was greater than in Argentina ($260.2 billion), in Colombia ($89.7 billion), in Venezuela ($67.3 billion), in Peru ($43.5 billion), in Uruguay ($18.6 billion), in Paraguay ($8.3 billion), and in Bolivia ($6.4 billion). The gross national income per capita in Brazil was greater than in Venezuela ($3.1 thousand), in Colombia ($2.5 thousand), in Peru ($1 808.1), in Paraguay ($1 755.9), and in Bolivia ($852.7); but less than in Argentina ($7.5 thousand) and in Uruguay ($5.8 thousand). The growth of gross national income in Brazil was less than in Argentina (4.8%), in Bolivia (4.3%), in Uruguay (3.8%), in Colombia (3.2%), in Peru (3.0%), in Venezuela (2.7%), and in Paraguay (2.2%).

Comparison with leaders. The Brazil's gross national income was less than in the United States ($7.5 trillion), in Japan ($4.4 trillion), in Germany ($2.2 trillion), in France ($1.4 trillion), and in the United Kingdom ($1.3 trillion). The Brazilian GNI per capita was less than in Japan ($34.7 thousand), in the United States ($28.5 thousand), in Germany ($27.0 thousand), in France ($24.3 thousand), and in the UK ($23.0 thousand). The growth of gross national income in Brazil was greater than in Japan (1.5%); but less than in the United States (3.4%), in France (2.2%), in the UK (2.0%), and in Germany (2.0%).

The 2000s

The gross national income of Brazil was $945.9 billion per year in the 2000s, ranked 10th in the world, and was on a par with Central America ($932.4 billion). The share in the world was 2.0%, and 5.7% in the Americas.

The GNI per capita in Brazil was $5 119.3 in the 2000s, ranked 86th in the world, and was on a par with Lebanon ($5.1 thousand), Dominica ($5.1 thousand). The GNI per capita in Brazil was less than gross national income per capita in the world ($7 165.2) by 28.6%, and was less than gross national income per capita in the Americas ($18 970.5) in 3.7 times.

The growth of gross national income in Brazil was 3.4% in the 2000s, ranked 116th in the world, and was on a par with Saint Kitts and Nevis (3.4%). The growth of GNI in Brazil (3.4%) was greater than growth of GNI in the world (3.0%), was greater than growth of gross national income in the Americas (2.1%).

Comparison with neighbors. The gross national income of Brazil was greater than in Argentina ($235.6 billion), in Venezuela ($171.9 billion), in Colombia ($145.5 billion), in Peru ($74.6 billion), in Uruguay ($20.1 billion), in Paraguay ($12.4 billion), and in Bolivia ($10.6 billion). The Brazilian gross national income per capita was greater than in Colombia ($3.4 thousand), in Peru ($2.7 thousand), in Paraguay ($2.2 thousand), and in Bolivia ($1 157.3); but less than in Venezuela ($6.6 thousand), in Argentina ($6.1 thousand), and in Uruguay ($6.0 thousand). The growth of gross national income in Brazil was greater than in Argentina (2.3%) and in Uruguay (1.7%); but less than in Peru (4.6%), in Paraguay (4.4%), in Venezuela (3.7%), in Colombia (3.6%), and in Bolivia (3.5%).

Comparison with leaders. The Brazilian gross national income was less than in the United States ($12.7 trillion), in Japan ($4.8 trillion), in Germany ($2.8 trillion), in China ($2.6 trillion), and in the UK ($2.3 trillion). The GNI per capita in Brazil was greater than in China ($1 950.5); but less than in the USA ($43.2 thousand), in the United Kingdom ($38.5 thousand), in Japan ($37.1 thousand), and in Germany ($34.2 thousand). The growth of GNI in Brazil was greater than in the USA (1.8%), in the United Kingdom (1.7%), in Germany (1.0%), and in Japan (0.62%); but less than in China (10.4%).

The 2010s

The gross national income of Brazil was $2.1 trillion per year in the 2010s, ranked 8th in the world, and was on a par with Italy ($2.1 trillion). The share in the world was 2.7%, and 8.3% in the Americas.

The gross national income per capita in Brazil was $10 378.3 in the 2010s, ranked 80th in the world, and was on a par with Costa Rica ($10.3 thousand), Malaysia ($10.2 thousand), Eastern Europe ($10.6 thousand). The gross national income per capita in Brazil was less than gross national income per capita in the world ($10 611.7) by 2.2%, and was less than GNI per capita in the Americas ($26 262.7) in 2.5 times.

The growth of GNI in Brazil was 1.3% in the 2010s, ranked 171st in the world, and was on a par with Croatia (1.3%), Haiti (1.3%). The growth of GNI in Brazil (1.3%) was less than growth of GNI in the world (3.1%), was less than growth of GNI in the Americas (2.3%).

Comparison with neighbors. The GNI of Brazil was 3.9 times higher than in Argentina ($538.9 billion), 6.6 times higher than in Colombia ($320.8 billion), 7.1 times higher than in Venezuela ($297.2 billion), 11.4 times higher than in Peru ($185.4 billion), 41.2 times higher than in Uruguay ($51.3 billion), 60.4 times higher than in Paraguay ($34.9 billion), and 68.7 times higher than in Bolivia ($30.8 billion). The Brazilian gross national income per capita was 2.4% higher than in Venezuela ($10.1 thousand), 53.7% higher than in Colombia ($6.8 thousand), 70.7% higher than in Peru ($6.1 thousand), 97.3% higher than in Paraguay ($5.3 thousand), and 3.6 times higher than in Bolivia ($2.9 thousand); but 31.0% lower than in Uruguay ($15.0 thousand) and 17.5% lower than in Argentina ($12.6 thousand). The growth of gross national income in Brazil was greater than in Argentina (1.2%) and in Venezuela (-9.8%); but less than in Bolivia (4.8%), in Peru (4.6%), in Paraguay (4.5%), in Colombia (3.8%), and in Uruguay (2.8%).

Comparison with leaders. The GNI of Brazil was 8.7 times lower than in the USA ($18.3 trillion), 5.0 times lower than in China ($10.5 trillion), 2.6 times lower than in Japan ($5.4 trillion), 43.7% lower than in Germany ($3.7 trillion), and 23.1% lower than in France ($2.7 trillion). The Brazil's GNI per capita was 39.0% higher than in China ($7.5 thousand); but 5.5 times lower than in the USA ($57.3 thousand), 4.4 times lower than in Germany ($45.8 thousand), 4.1 times lower than in Japan ($42.2 thousand), and 4.0 times lower than in France ($41.4 thousand). The growth of gross national income in Brazil was less than in China (7.7%), in the United States (2.5%), in Germany (2.0%), in Japan (1.4%), and in France (1.4%).

Part II. Structure

	The 2010s
agriculture	5.1%
industry	18.1%
construction	5.8%
trade	15.5%
transportation	7.9%
services	47.5%

Chapter IV. Agriculture

Agriculture, hunting, forestry, fishing (ISIC A-B)

The value of agriculture in Brazil enlarged from $10.8 billion per year in the 1970s to $95.1 billion per year in the 2010s, that is by $84.3 billion or 8.8 times. The change occurred at $52.6 billion due to a 2.2-fold increase in prices, as also at $21.8 billion due to a 2.1-fold increase in productivity, as well as at $9.9 billion due to the increase in population. The average annual growth in agriculture is 3.5%. The minimum value of agriculture was in 1970 at $3.7 billion. The maximum value of agriculture was in 2011 at $113.6 billion.

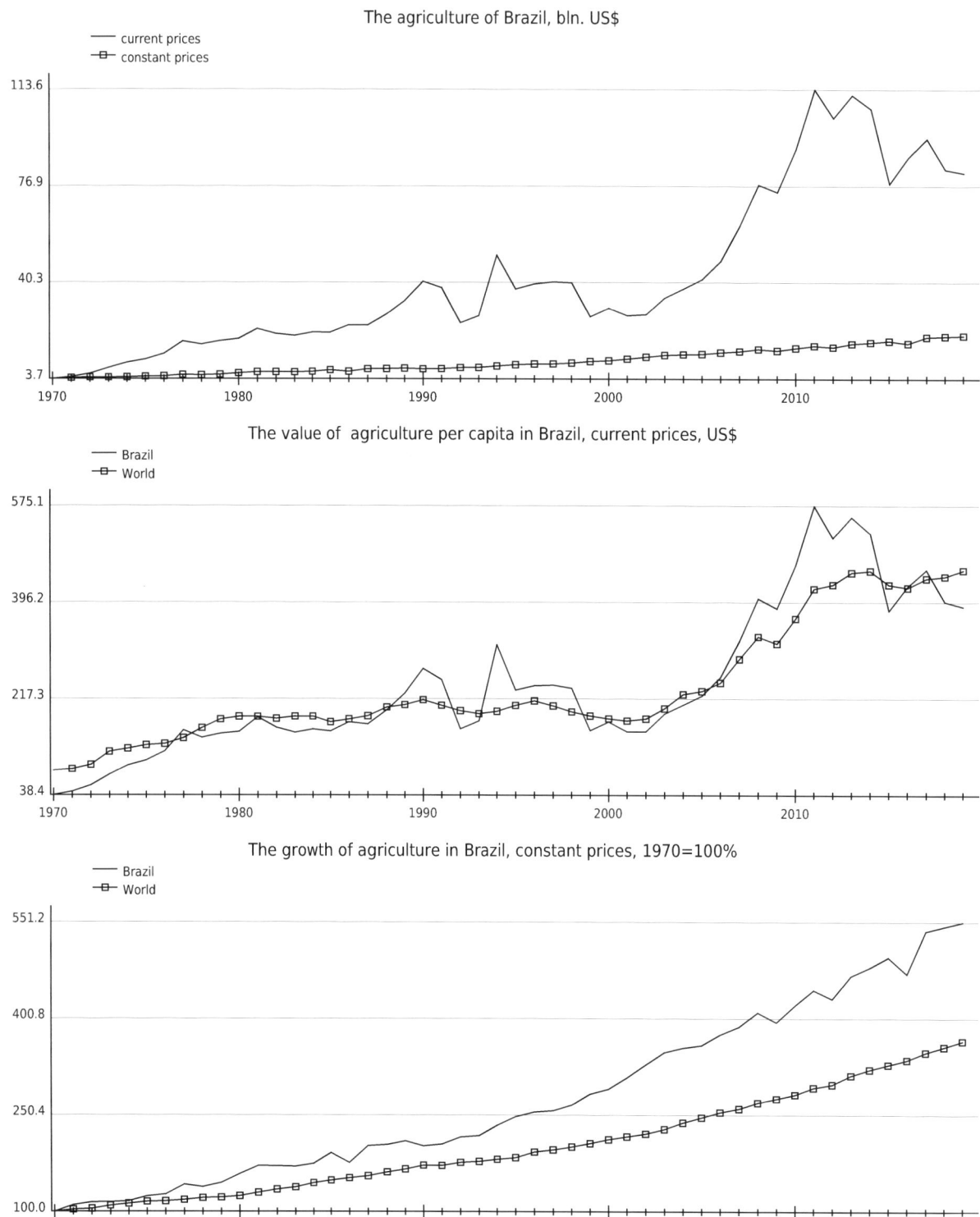

Chapter IV. Agriculture

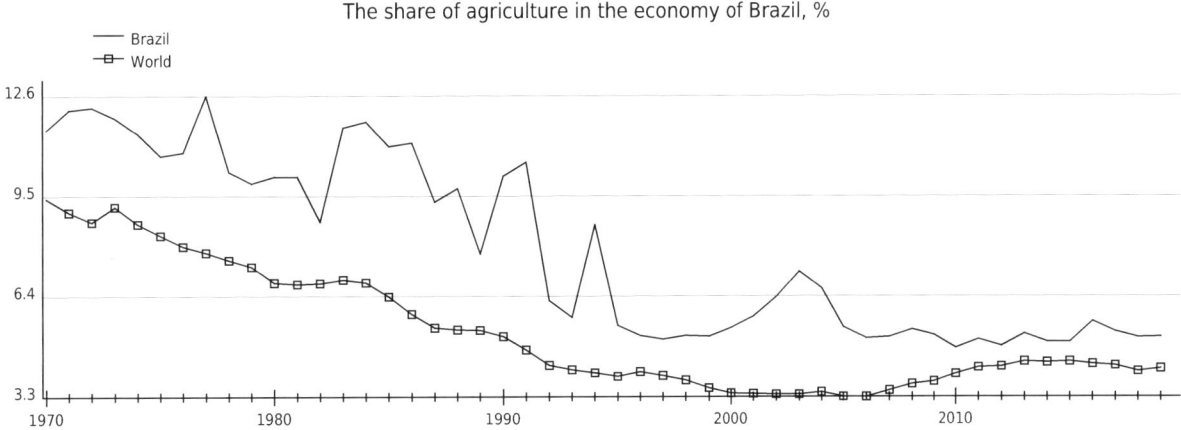

The 1970s

The value of agriculture in Brazil was $10.8 billion per year in the 1970s, ranked 11th in the world. The share in the world was 2.1%, and 12.2% in the Americas.

The share of agriculture in the economy of Brazil was 11.1% in the 1970s, ranked 112th in the world, and was on a par with Saint Kitts and Nevis (11.1%).

The value of agriculture per capita in Brazil was $101.8 in the 1970s, ranked 97th in the world, and was on a par with the Philippines ($101.8), Senegal ($101.3), Morocco ($100.9). The value of agriculture per capita in Brazil was less than agriculture per capita in the world ($127.6) by 20.3%, and was less than agriculture per capita in the Americas ($158.1) by 35.6%.

The growth of agriculture in Brazil was 4.2% in the 1970s, ranked 54th in the world, and was on a par with Thailand (4.2%). The growth of agriculture in Brazil (4.2%) was greater than growth of agriculture in the world (2.2%), was greater than growth of agriculture in the Americas (1.9%).

Comparison with neighbors. The value of agriculture in Brazil was greater than in Argentina ($3.9 billion), in Colombia ($3.3 billion), in Peru ($1.5 billion), in Venezuela ($1.5 billion), in Uruguay ($613.0 million), in Bolivia ($409.3 million), and in Paraguay ($331.4 million). The value added of agriculture per capita in Brazil was greater than in Peru ($100.6) and in Bolivia ($82.6); but less than in Uruguay ($215.9), in Argentina ($151.6), in Colombia ($137.0), in Paraguay ($119.7), and in Venezuela ($114.0). The growth of agriculture in Brazil was greater than in Venezuela (3.1%), in Argentina (2.9%), in Peru (0.064%), and in Uruguay (-0.95%); but less than in Paraguay (6.5%), in Colombia (4.6%), and in Bolivia (4.5%).

Comparison with leaders. The sector of agriculture in Brazil was less than in the USSR ($88.7 billion), in China ($49.5 billion), in the United States ($42.6 billion), in India ($36.0 billion), and in Japan ($25.8 billion). The agriculture per capita in Brazil was greater than in India ($58.3) and in China ($54.2); but less than in the USSR ($351.8), in Japan ($231.3), and in the United States ($195.0). The growth of agriculture in Brazil was greater than in China (2.4%), in Japan (0.52%), in the USA (0.34%), and in India (0.30%); but less than in the USSR (7.0%).

The 1980s

The sector of agriculture in Brazil was $23.4 billion per year in the 1980s, ranked 9th in the world. The share in the world was 2.6%, and 14.9% in the Americas.

The share of agriculture in the economy of Brazil was 9.8% in the 1980s, ranked 110th in the world, and was on a par with Congo (9.8%), the Marshall Islands (9.7%).

The sector of agriculture per capita in Brazil was $175.1 in the 1980s, ranked 88th in the world, and was on a par with the Dominican Republic ($177.5), the Seychelles ($179.4). The Brazilian agriculture per capita was less than agriculture per capita in the world ($186.6) by 6.1%, and was less than agriculture per capita in the Americas ($237.6) by 26.3%.

The growth of agriculture in Brazil was 3.8% in the 1980s, ranked 43rd in the world, and was on a par with Mali (3.7%), Kenya (3.7%), Asia (3.8%). The growth of agriculture in Brazil (3.8%) was greater than growth of agriculture in the world (3.1%), was greater than growth of agriculture in the Americas (2.6%).

Comparison with neighbors. The Brazilian agriculture was greater than in Argentina ($7.1 billion), in Colombia ($6.3 billion), in Venezuela ($3.6 billion), in Peru ($2.2 billion), in Paraguay ($923.4 million), in Uruguay ($909.6 million), and in Bolivia ($883.9 million). The value of agriculture per capita in Brazil was greater than in Bolivia ($144.2) and in Peru ($113.5); but less than in Uruguay ($303.0), in Paraguay ($254.2), in Argentina ($235.9), in Colombia ($212.8), and in Venezuela ($212.6). The growth of agriculture in Brazil was greater than in Colombia (2.6%), in Venezuela (2.4%), in Peru (2.2%), in Uruguay (1.7%), in Bolivia (1.4%), and in Argentina (-0.12%); but less than in Paraguay (4.6%).

Comparison with leaders. The value added of agriculture in Brazil was less than in the USSR ($125.8 billion), in China ($94.9 billion), in India ($70.4 billion), in the USA ($68.7 billion), and in Japan ($49.7 billion). The value of agriculture per capita in Brazil was greater than in India ($90.7) and in China ($88.5); but less than in the USSR ($457.2), in Japan ($410.0), and in the USA ($286.8). The growth of agriculture in Brazil was greater than in the USA (3.7%), in the USSR (2.8%), and in Japan (0.41%); but less than in China (5.3%) and in India (4.4%).

The 1990s

The value of agriculture in Brazil was $36.8 billion per year in the 1990s, ranked 5th in the world, and was on a par with Italy ($36.3 billion), Russia ($36.1 billion). The share in the world was 3.2%, and 16.5% in the Americas.

The share of agriculture in the economy of Brazil was 6.4% in the 1990s, ranked 139th in the world.

The Brazil's agriculture per capita was $228.7 in the 1990s, ranked 90th in the world, and was on a par with Central America ($230.3), Colombia ($226.4), Eastern Europe ($226.3). The value added of agriculture per capita in Brazil was greater than agriculture per capita in the world ($199.8) by 14.5%, and was less than agriculture per capita in the Americas ($288.9) by 20.8%.

The growth of agriculture in Brazil was 3% in the 1990s, ranked 67th in the world, and was on a par with Senegal (3.0%), Iraq (3.0%), Western Asia (3.0%). The growth of agriculture in Brazil (3.0%) was greater than growth of agriculture in the world (2.2%), was greater than growth of agriculture in the Americas (2.4%).

Comparison with neighbors. The value added of agriculture in Brazil was greater than in Argentina ($12.8 billion), in Colombia ($8.2 billion), in Peru ($3.7 billion), in Venezuela ($3.6 billion), in Uruguay ($1.3 billion), in Paraguay ($1.2 billion), and in Bolivia ($954.3 million). The Brazilian agriculture per capita was greater than in Colombia ($226.4), in Venezuela ($165.1), in Peru ($152.8), and in Bolivia ($126.4); but less than in Uruguay ($412.5), in Argentina ($370.0), and in Paraguay ($244.9). The growth of agriculture in Brazil was greater than in Paraguay (2.6%), in Uruguay (2.5%), in Colombia (1.5%), and in Venezuela (1.4%); but less than in Peru (3.8%), in Argentina (3.8%), and in Bolivia (3.1%).

Comparison with leaders. The value of agriculture in Brazil was greater than in Italy ($36.3 billion); but less than in China ($139.0 billion), in the United States ($96.1 billion), in India ($91.4 billion), and in Japan ($78.9 billion). The Brazilian agriculture per capita was greater than in China ($112.7) and in India ($95.6); but less than in Italy ($636.4), in Japan ($625.5), and in the USA ($363.4). The growth of agriculture in Brazil was greater than in India (2.8%), in the USA (2.6%), in Italy (2.4%), and in Japan (-1.8%); but less than in China (4.3%).

The 2000s

The sector of agriculture in Brazil was $46.2 billion per year in the 2000s, ranked 6th in the world, and was on a par with Northern Africa ($47.0 billion). The share in the world was 3.0%, and 16.1% in the Americas.

The share of agriculture in the economy of Brazil was 5.6% in the 2000s, ranked 123rd in the world, and was on a par with Angola (5.6%).

The sector of agriculture per capita in Brazil was $250.3 in the 2000s, ranked 100th in the world, and was on a par with Cabo Verde ($251.4), Papua New Guinea ($248.4), Eastern Asia ($248.4). The sector of agriculture per capita in Brazil was greater than agriculture per capita in the world ($240.3) by 4.1%, and was less than agriculture per capita in the Americas ($327.5) by 23.6%.

The growth of agriculture in Brazil was 3.4% in the 2000s, ranked 64th in the world, and was on a par with Indonesia (3.4%), São Tomé and Príncipe (3.4%). The growth of agriculture in Brazil (3.4%) was greater than growth of agriculture in the world (3.0%), was greater than growth of agriculture in the Americas (2.7%).

Comparison with neighbors. The value of agriculture in Brazil was greater than in Argentina ($15.9 billion), in Colombia ($10.9 billion), in Venezuela ($7.4 billion), in Peru ($5.7 billion), in Uruguay ($1.7 billion), in Paraguay ($1.5 billion), and in Bolivia ($1.3 billion). The

Chapter IV. Agriculture

value of agriculture per capita in Brazil was greater than in Peru ($205.2) and in Bolivia ($140.0); but less than in Uruguay ($503.6), in Argentina ($409.8), in Venezuela ($282.1), in Paraguay ($263.9), and in Colombia ($258.3). The growth of agriculture in Brazil was greater than in Paraguay (3.2%), in Bolivia (3.1%), in Venezuela (2.8%), in Colombia (2.2%), in Uruguay (1.0%), and in Argentina (-0.54%); but less than in Peru (3.7%).

Comparison with leaders. The sector of agriculture in Brazil was less than in China ($297.7 billion), in India ($147.6 billion), in the USA ($122.5 billion), in Japan ($57.1 billion), and in Nigeria ($47.6 billion). The value of agriculture per capita in Brazil was greater than in China ($224.5) and in India ($129.7); but less than in Japan ($445.6), in the United States ($416.9), and in Nigeria ($346.4). The growth of agriculture in Brazil was greater than in India (2.0%) and in Japan (-1.3%); but less than in Nigeria (10.1%), in China (4.0%), and in the United States (3.6%).

The 2010s

The sector of agriculture in Brazil was $95.1 billion per year in the 2010s, ranked 6th in the world, and was on a par with Nigeria ($95.8 billion). The share in the world was 3.0%, and 19.6% in the Americas.

The share of agriculture in the economy of Brazil was 5.1% in the 2010s, ranked 123rd in the world, and was on a par with Lesotho (5.2%).

The sector of agriculture per capita in Brazil was $467.2 in the 2010s, ranked 69th in the world, and was on a par with Japan ($466.2), Palau ($464.4), Romania ($463.7). The value of agriculture per capita in Brazil was greater than agriculture per capita in the world ($432.1) by 8.1%, and was less than agriculture per capita in the Americas ($498.8) by 6.3%.

The growth of agriculture in Brazil was 3.4% in the 2010s, ranked 58th in the world, and was on a par with Zimbabwe (3.4%), Malawi (3.4%), DR Congo (3.4%). The growth of agriculture in Brazil (3.4%) was greater than growth of agriculture in the world (2.9%), was greater than growth of agriculture in the Americas (2.2%).

Comparison with neighbors. The value of agriculture in Brazil was 2.8 times higher than in Argentina ($34.4 billion), 4.8 times higher than in Colombia ($20.0 billion), 6.0 times higher than in Venezuela ($15.9 billion), 7.1 times higher than in Peru ($13.4 billion), 23.4 times higher than in Paraguay ($4.1 billion), 26.7 times higher than in Uruguay ($3.6 billion), and 27.6 times higher than in Bolivia ($3.4 billion). The sector of agriculture per capita in Brazil was 6.0% higher than in Peru ($440.6), 11.2% higher than in Colombia ($420.1), and 46.3% higher than in Bolivia ($319.4); but 2.2 times lower than in Uruguay ($1 045.1), 41.8% lower than in Argentina ($802.4), 23.7% lower than in Paraguay ($612.0), and 13.7% lower than in Venezuela ($541.6). The growth of agriculture in Brazil was greater than in Colombia (3.2%), in Peru (3.1%), in Uruguay (0.98%), and in Venezuela (-12.1%); but less than in Paraguay (6.4%), in Bolivia (4.2%), and in Argentina (4.0%).

Comparison with leaders. The Brazil's agriculture was 9.3 times lower than in China ($886.2 billion), 3.8 times lower than in India ($363.4 billion), 47.3% lower than in the United States ($180.3 billion), 23.4% lower than in Indonesia ($124.1 billion), and 0.71% lower than in Nigeria ($95.8 billion). The sector of agriculture per capita in Brazil was 67.4% higher than in India ($279.1); but 26.1% lower than in China ($631.9), 17.2% lower than in the United States ($564.3), 12.6% lower than in Nigeria ($534.6), and 3.4% lower than in Indonesia ($483.6). The growth of agriculture in Brazil was greater than in the United States (2.0%); but less than in India (4.1%), in Indonesia (3.9%), in China (3.8%), and in Nigeria (3.6%).

Chapter V. Industry

Mining, Manufacturing, Utilities (ISIC C-E)

The value of industry in Brazil grew up from $32.3 billion per year in the 1970s to $334.5 billion per year in the 2010s, that is by $302.2 billion or 10.4 times. The change occurred at $256.3 billion due to a 4.3-fold increase in prices, as also at $16.3 billion due to a 1.3-fold increase in productivity, as well as at $29.6 billion due to the growth in population. The average annual growth in industry is 2.8%. The minimum value of industry was in 1970 at $9.6 billion. The maximum value of industry was in 2011 at $464.8 billion.

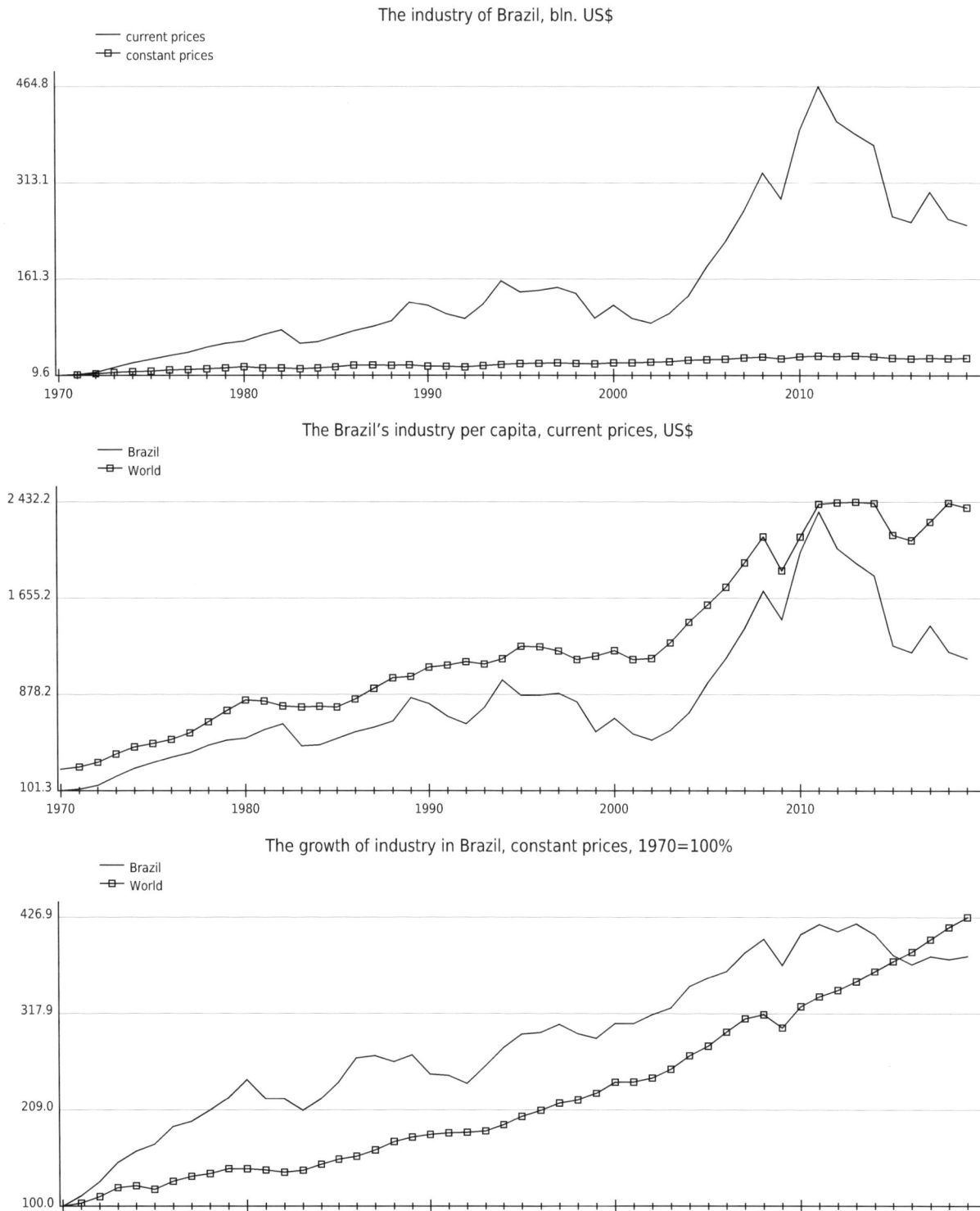

Chapter V. Industry

The 1970s

The value added of industry in Brazil was $32.3 billion per year in the 1970s, ranked 10th in the world. The share in the world was 1.7%, and 5.3% in the Americas.

The share of industry in the economy of Brazil was 33.1% in the 1970s, ranked 39th in the world, and was on a par with Peru (33.0%).

The value of industry per capita in Brazil was $304.0 in the 1970s, ranked 73rd in the world, and was on a par with Guyana ($303.9), the Dominican Republic ($302.6), the Caribbean ($311.5). The value added of industry per capita in Brazil was less than industry per capita in the world ($480.5) by 36.7%, and was less than industry per capita in the Americas ($1 091.1) in 3.6 times.

The growth of industry in Brazil was 9.3% in the 1970s, ranked 23rd in the world, and was on a par with Indonesia (9.3%). The growth of industry in Brazil (9.3%) was greater than growth of industry in the world (4.0%), was greater than growth of industry in the Americas (3.2%).

Comparison with neighbors. The industry of Brazil was greater than in Argentina ($16.8 billion), in Venezuela ($13.1 billion), in Colombia ($4.8 billion), in Peru ($3.2 billion), in Uruguay ($884.8 million), in Bolivia ($575.7 million), and in Paraguay ($569.4 million). The industry per capita in Brazil was greater than in Peru ($210.2), in Paraguay ($205.6), in Colombia ($201.8), and in Bolivia ($116.2); but less than in Venezuela ($1 001.8), in Argentina ($655.8), and in Uruguay ($311.6). The growth of industry in Brazil was greater than in Paraguay (8.0%), in Colombia (5.8%), in Peru (5.4%), in Bolivia (4.9%), in Uruguay (3.4%), in Argentina (2.4%), and in Venezuela (0.44%).

Comparison with leaders. The value of industry in Brazil was less than in the United States ($450.4 billion), in the USSR ($248.8 billion), in Japan ($185.6 billion), in Germany ($158.4 billion), and in the United Kingdom ($72.6 billion). The Brazilian industry per capita was less than in the USA ($2.1 thousand), in Germany ($2.0 thousand), in Japan ($1 666.5), in the United Kingdom ($1 295.1), and in the USSR ($986.6). The growth of industry in Brazil was greater than in the USSR (5.2%), in Japan (4.5%), in the United States (2.4%), in Germany (2.1%), and in the United Kingdom (1.9%).

The 1980s

The industry of Brazil was $79.8 billion per year in the 1980s, ranked 11th in the world. The share in the world was 1.9%, and 5.8% in the Americas.

The share of industry in the economy of Brazil was 33.5% in the 1980s, ranked 32nd in the world, and was on a par with Hungary (33.8%).

The industry per capita in Brazil was $596.7 in the 1980s, ranked 70th in the world, and was on a par with Chile ($595.1), Nigeria ($585.9), Eastern Asia ($607.7). The value added of industry per capita in Brazil was less than industry per capita in the world ($861.8) by 30.8%, and was less than industry per capita in the Americas ($2 085.6) in 3.5 times.

The growth of industry in Brazil was 2% in the 1980s, ranked 113th in the world. The growth of industry in Brazil (2.0%) was less than growth of industry in the world (2.3%), was greater than growth of industry in the Americas (1.9%).

Comparison with neighbors. The sector of industry in Brazil was greater than in Argentina ($28.7 billion), in Venezuela ($26.3 billion), in Colombia ($13.0 billion), in Peru ($8.1 billion), in Paraguay ($1.9 billion), in Uruguay ($1.9 billion), and in Bolivia ($1.1 billion). The value added of industry per capita in Brazil was greater than in Paraguay ($535.2), in Colombia ($437.9), in Peru ($414.7), and in Bolivia ($181.7); but less than in Venezuela ($1 533.2), in Argentina ($955.5), and in Uruguay ($616.5). The growth of industry in Brazil was greater than in Venezuela (0.60%), in Uruguay (-0.24%), in Bolivia (-1.4%), in Argentina (-1.5%), and in Peru (-1.6%); but less than in Colombia (4.9%) and in Paraguay (3.3%).

Comparison with leaders. The Brazil's industry was less than in the United States ($1.0 trillion), in Japan ($566.4 billion), in the USSR ($305.7 billion), in Germany ($297.5 billion), and in the United Kingdom ($171.2 billion). The value of industry per capita in Brazil was less than in Japan ($4.7 thousand), in the United States ($4.2 thousand), in Germany ($3.8 thousand), in the United Kingdom ($3.0 thousand), and in the USSR ($1 110.8). The growth of industry in Brazil was greater than in the United States (1.9%), in the United Kingdom (1.4%), and in Germany (1.2%); but less than in the USSR (5.3%) and in Japan (4.2%).

The 1990s

The sector of industry in Brazil was $127.7 billion per year in the 1990s, ranked 10th in the world, and was on a par with Mexico ($125.8 billion). The share in the world was 1.9%, and 6.1% in the Americas.

The share of industry in the economy of Brazil was 22.2% in the 1990s, ranked 103rd in the world, and was on a par with Ivory Coast (22.2%), Vietnam (22.3%), Jordan (22.1%).

The industry per capita in Brazil was $794.7 in the 1990s, ranked 74th in the world, and was on a par with Eastern Europe ($786.1), Lebanon ($780.8). The industry per capita in Brazil was less than industry per capita in the world ($1 175.6) by 32.4%, and was less than industry per capita in the Americas ($2 704.1) in 3.4 times.

The growth of industry in Brazil was 0.7% in the 1990s, ranked 149th in the world. The growth of industry in Brazil (0.67%) was less than growth of industry in the world (2.5%), was less than growth of industry in the Americas (2.8%).

Comparison with neighbors. The industry of Brazil was greater than in Argentina ($52.9 billion), in Venezuela ($27.7 billion), in Colombia ($21.0 billion), in Peru ($10.4 billion), in Uruguay ($3.5 billion), in Paraguay ($2.9 billion), and in Bolivia ($1.7 billion). The industry per capita in Brazil was greater than in Paraguay ($617.9), in Colombia ($581.7), in Peru ($433.7), and in Bolivia ($219.2); but less than in Argentina ($1 530.5), in Venezuela ($1 277.0), and in Uruguay ($1 089.4). The growth of industry in Brazil was greater than in Uruguay (0.55%); but less than in Argentina (4.3%), in Bolivia (4.0%), in Venezuela (3.1%), in Peru (2.8%), in Colombia (2.2%), and in Paraguay (1.3%).

Comparison with leaders. The industry of Brazil was less than in the USA ($1.5 trillion), in Japan ($1.2 trillion), in Germany ($534.0 billion), in China ($285.9 billion), and in the United Kingdom ($268.6 billion). The Brazil's industry per capita was greater than in China ($231.9); but less than in Japan ($9.4 thousand), in Germany ($6.6 thousand), in the United States ($5.7 thousand), and in the United Kingdom ($4.6 thousand). The growth of industry in Brazil was greater than in Germany (0.33%); but less than in China (13.1%), in the USA (2.8%), in Japan (1.3%), and in the UK (1.2%).

The 2000s

The Brazilian industry was $183.8 billion per year in the 2000s, ranked 12th in the world, and was on a par with India ($179.9 billion). The share in the world was 1.8%, and 6.0% in the Americas.

The share of industry in the economy of Brazil was 22.2% in the 2000s, ranked 93rd in the world, and was on a par with Turkey (22.3%).

The value added of industry per capita in Brazil was $994.9 in the 2000s, ranked 91st in the world, and was on a par with Saint Kitts and Nevis ($987.6), Costa Rica ($983.8). The Brazil's industry per capita was less than industry per capita in the world ($1 573.8) by 36.8%, and was less than industry per capita in the Americas ($3 499.5) in 3.5 times.

The growth of industry in Brazil was 2.5% in the 2000s, ranked 102nd in the world. The growth of industry in Brazil (2.5%) was less than growth of industry in the world (2.9%), was greater than growth of industry in the Americas (1.4%).

Comparison with neighbors. The sector of industry in Brazil was greater than in Venezuela ($68.1 billion), in Argentina ($54.7 billion), in Colombia ($38.4 billion), in Peru ($22.7 billion), in Paraguay ($4.8 billion), in Uruguay ($3.5 billion), and in Bolivia ($2.7 billion). The industry per capita in Brazil was greater than in Colombia ($907.6), in Paraguay ($841.5), in Peru ($819.8), and in Bolivia ($299.1); but less than in Venezuela ($2.6 thousand), in Argentina ($1 413.0), and in Uruguay ($1 038.8). The growth of industry in Brazil was greater than in Uruguay (2.3%), in Argentina (2.2%), and in Venezuela (0.85%); but less than in Peru (5.2%), in Bolivia (4.8%), in

Chapter V. Industry

Paraguay (4.2%), and in Colombia (3.0%).

Comparison with leaders. The industry of Brazil was less than in the United States ($2.1 trillion), in Japan ($1.1 trillion), in China ($1.1 trillion), in Germany ($629.4 billion), and in the United Kingdom ($345.1 billion). The sector of industry per capita in Brazil was greater than in China ($795.3); but less than in Japan ($8.8 thousand), in Germany ($7.7 thousand), in the USA ($7.1 thousand), and in the UK ($5.7 thousand). The growth of industry in Brazil was greater than in the USA (1.5%), in Germany (0.19%), in Japan (0.15%), and in the United Kingdom (-1.1%); but less than in China (11.1%).

The 2010s

The value of industry in Brazil was $334.5 billion per year in the 2010s, ranked 12th in the world, and was on a par with France ($334.8 billion), Saudi Arabia ($336.0 billion). The share in the world was 2.0%, and 7.9% in the Americas.

The share of industry in the economy of Brazil was 18.1% in the 2010s, ranked 119th in the world, and was on a par with Australasia (18.1%), Oceania (18.1%), Pakistan (18.2%).

The industry per capita in Brazil was $1 643.4 in the 2010s, ranked 83rd in the world, and was on a par with Costa Rica ($1 658.1), Colombia ($1 625.5), Peru ($1 663.8). The value of industry per capita in Brazil was less than industry per capita in the world ($2 320.9) by 29.2%, and was less than industry per capita in the Americas ($4 354.8) in 2.6 times.

The growth of industry in Brazil was 0.3% in the 2010s, ranked 174th in the world. The growth of industry in Brazil (0.27%) was less than growth of industry in the world (3.5%), was less than growth of industry in the Americas (1.8%).

Comparison with neighbors. The value of industry in Brazil was 3.2 times higher than in Argentina ($105.9 billion), 3.4 times higher than in Venezuela ($97.5 billion), 4.3 times higher than in Colombia ($77.2 billion), 6.6 times higher than in Peru ($50.7 billion), 32.8 times higher than in Paraguay ($10.2 billion), 41.7 times higher than in Uruguay ($8.0 billion), and 43.1 times higher than in Bolivia ($7.8 billion). The Brazilian industry per capita was 1.1% higher than in Colombia ($1 625.5), 7.0% higher than in Paraguay ($1 535.8), and 2.3 times higher than in Bolivia ($719.7); but 2.0 times lower than in Venezuela ($3.3 thousand), 33.5% lower than in Argentina ($2.5 thousand), 30.2% lower than in Uruguay ($2.4 thousand), and 1.2% lower than in Peru ($1 663.8). The growth of industry in Brazil was greater than in Argentina (-0.33%) and in Venezuela (-5.9%); but less than in Bolivia (3.4%), in Paraguay (3.2%), in Peru (3.0%), in Colombia (2.1%), and in Uruguay (1.7%).

Comparison with leaders. The value of industry in Brazil was 11.0 times lower than in China ($3.7 trillion), 8.2 times lower than in the United States ($2.7 trillion), 3.6 times lower than in Japan ($1.2 trillion), 2.5 times lower than in Germany ($840.0 billion), and 24.6% lower than in India ($443.4 billion). The value added of industry per capita in Brazil was 4.8 times higher than in India ($340.6); but 6.2 times lower than in Germany ($10.3 thousand), 5.7 times lower than in Japan ($9.3 thousand), 5.2 times lower than in the USA ($8.6 thousand), and 37.4% lower than in China ($2.6 thousand). The growth of industry in Brazil was less than in China (7.5%), in India (6.5%), in Germany (3.2%), in Japan (2.6%), and in the United States (2.2%).

Chapter 5.1. Manufacturing

(ISIC D)

The sector of manufacturing in Brazil increased from $29.6 billion per year in the 1970s to $232.9 billion per year in the 2010s, that is by $203.3 billion or 7.9 times. The change occurred at $167.0 billion due to a 3.5-fold increase in prices, as also at $9.1 billion due to a 1.2-fold increase in productivity, as well as at $27.1 billion due to the increase in population. The average annual growth in manufacturing is 2.5%. The minimum value of manufacturing was in 1970 at $8.7 billion. The maximum value of manufacturing was in 2011 at $308.3 billion.

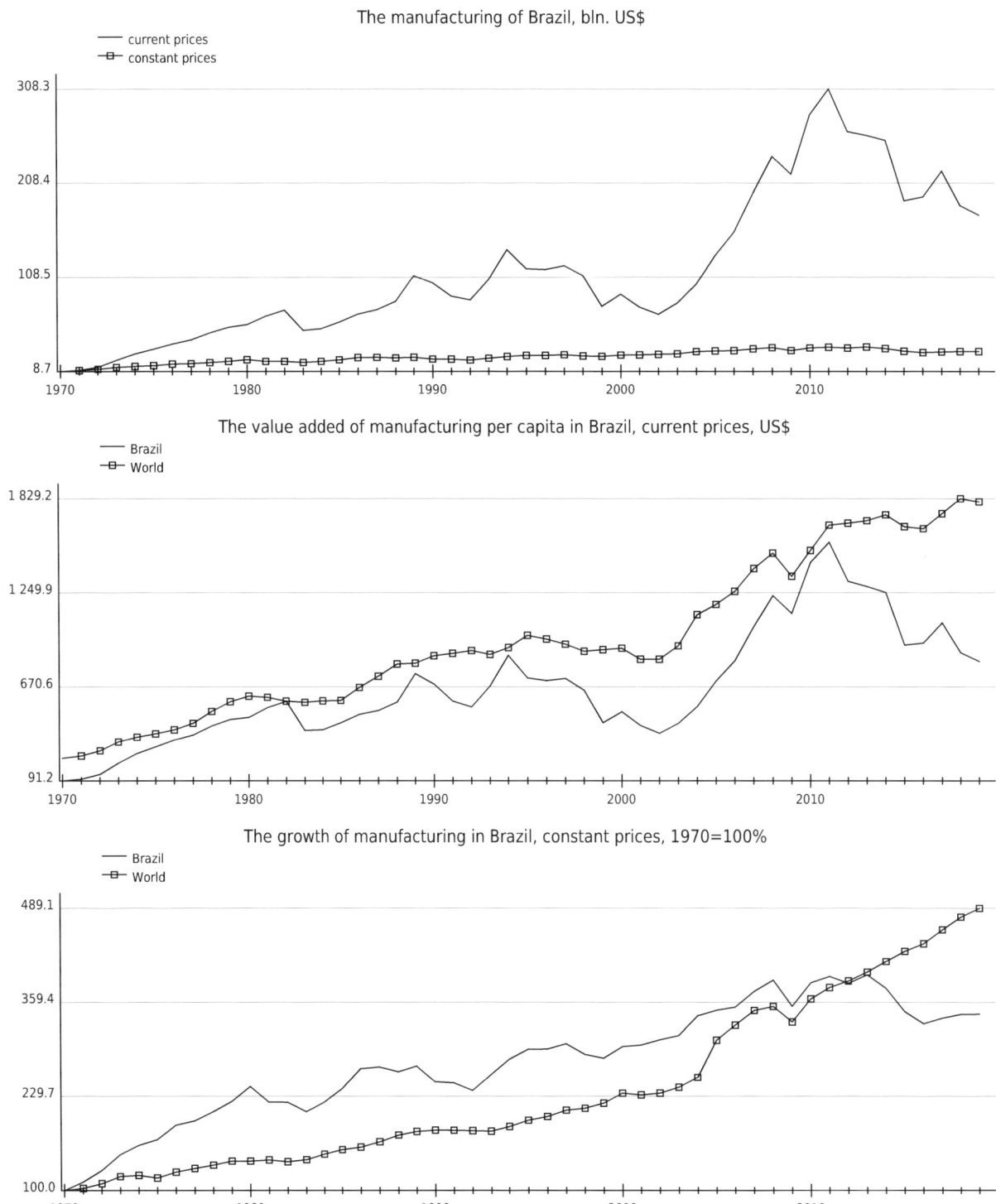

Chapter 5.1. Manufacturing

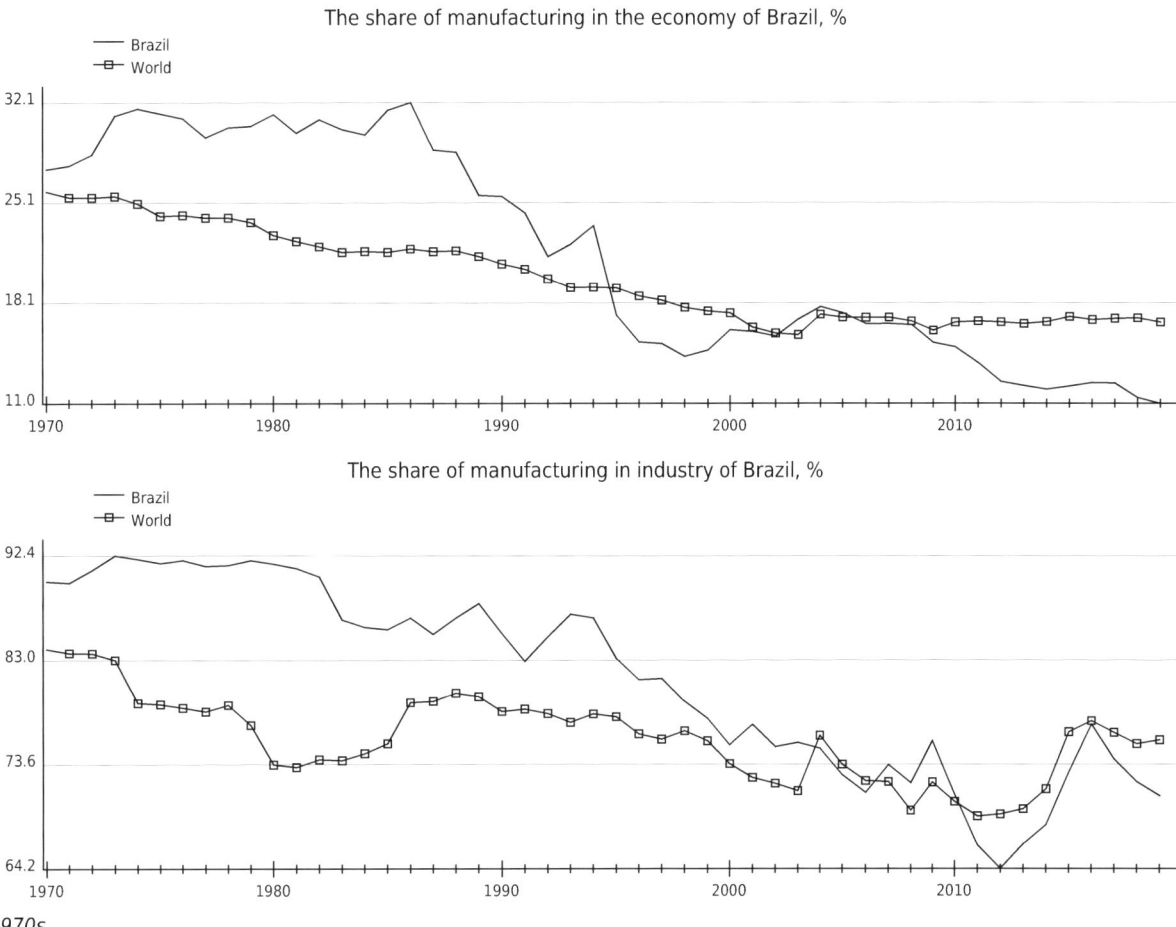

The 1970s

The sector of manufacturing in Brazil was $29.6 billion per year in the 1970s, ranked 9th in the world. The share in the world was 1.9%, and 5.9% in the Americas.

The share of manufacturing in the economy of Brazil was 30.4% in the 1970s, ranked 11th in the world, and was on a par with Paraguay (30.1%).

The value of manufacturing per capita in Brazil was $278.8 in the 1970s, ranked 57th in the world, and was on a par with Central America ($279.6), South Africa ($282.8), the Dominican Republic ($273.2). The Brazil's manufacturing per capita was less than manufacturing per capita in the world ($383.2) by 27.3%, and was less than manufacturing per capita in the Americas ($896.7) in 3.2 times.

The growth of manufacturing in Brazil was 9.3% in the 1970s, ranked 24th in the world. The growth of manufacturing in Brazil (9.3%) was greater than growth of manufacturing in the world (3.8%), was greater than growth of manufacturing in the Americas (3.6%).

Comparison with neighbors. The Brazil's manufacturing was greater than in Argentina ($15.4 billion), in Venezuela ($7.4 billion), in Colombia ($4.4 billion), in Peru ($1.4 billion), in Uruguay ($817.2 million), in Paraguay ($550.4 million), and in Bolivia ($267.5 million). The manufacturing per capita in Brazil was greater than in Paraguay ($198.8), in Colombia ($183.0), in Peru ($94.5), and in Bolivia ($54.0); but less than in Argentina ($598.3), in Venezuela ($569.3), and in Uruguay ($287.8). The growth of manufacturing in Brazil was greater than in Paraguay (7.8%), in Colombia (6.5%), in Bolivia (5.8%), in Venezuela (5.5%), in Uruguay (3.4%), in Peru (3.0%), and in Argentina (2.2%).

Comparison with leaders. The Brazilian manufacturing was less than in the United States ($378.0 billion), in the USSR ($248.8 billion), in Japan ($169.3 billion), in Germany ($138.0 billion), and in France ($64.5 billion). The manufacturing per capita in Brazil was less than in Germany ($1 752.1), in the USA ($1 731.8), in Japan ($1 520.6), in France ($1 203.0), and in the USSR ($986.6). The growth of manufacturing in Brazil was greater than in the USSR (5.2%), in Japan (4.5%), in France (3.5%), in the United States (2.7%), and in Germany (2.1%).

The 1980s

The value of manufacturing in Brazil was $70.1 billion per year in the 1980s, ranked 8th in the world. The share in the world was 2.2%, and 6.6% in the Americas.

The share of manufacturing in the economy of Brazil was 29.4% in the 1980s, ranked 9th in the world, and was on a par with Paraguay (29.2%).

The value of manufacturing per capita in Brazil was $524.4 in the 1980s, ranked 57th in the world, and was on a par with South America ($516.2), Hungary ($532.8), South Africa ($533.5). The manufacturing per capita in Brazil was less than manufacturing per capita in the world ($661.2) by 20.7%, and was less than manufacturing per capita in the Americas ($1 597.5) in 3.0 times.

The growth of manufacturing in Brazil was 2% in the 1980s, ranked 118th in the world, and was on a par with Central America (2.0%), DR Congo (2.0%), Costa Rica (2.0%). The growth of manufacturing in Brazil (2.0%) was less than growth of manufacturing in the world (2.6%), was greater than growth of manufacturing in the Americas (1.8%).

Comparison with neighbors. The manufacturing of Brazil was greater than in Argentina ($24.7 billion), in Venezuela ($16.4 billion), in Colombia ($10.5 billion), in Peru ($3.6 billion), in Paraguay ($1.8 billion), in Uruguay ($1.7 billion), and in Bolivia ($557.8 million). The Brazil's manufacturing per capita was greater than in Paraguay ($507.9), in Colombia ($352.7), in Peru ($182.8), and in Bolivia ($91.0); but less than in Venezuela ($955.2), in Argentina ($822.5), and in Uruguay ($554.7). The growth of manufacturing in Brazil was greater than in Venezuela (1.5%), in Uruguay (-0.58%), in Peru (-0.73%), in Bolivia (-1.7%), and in Argentina (-2.0%); but less than in Paraguay (3.2%) and in Colombia (2.6%).

Comparison with leaders. The manufacturing of Brazil was less than in the USA ($789.4 billion), in Japan ($501.0 billion), in the USSR ($305.7 billion), in Germany ($258.7 billion), and in Italy ($134.1 billion). The Brazilian manufacturing per capita was less than in Japan ($4.1 thousand), in Germany ($3.3 thousand), in the United States ($3.3 thousand), in Italy ($2.4 thousand), and in the USSR ($1 110.8). The growth of manufacturing in Brazil was greater than in the United States (1.9%) and in Germany (1.2%); but less than in the USSR (5.3%), in Japan (4.4%), and in Italy (2.5%).

The 1990s

The manufacturing of Brazil was $106.1 billion per year in the 1990s, ranked 8th in the world. The share in the world was 2.0%, and 6.3% in the Americas.

The share of manufacturing in the economy of Brazil was 18.4% in the 1990s, ranked 65th in the world, and was on a par with New Zealand (18.4%), Malawi (18.5%), India (18.5%).

The manufacturing per capita in Brazil was $660.3 in the 1990s, ranked 61st in the world, and was on a par with Poland ($659.9), South America ($653.1), Mauritius ($670.8). The manufacturing per capita in Brazil was less than manufacturing per capita in the world ($908.4) by 27.3%, and was less than manufacturing per capita in the Americas ($2 172.9) in 3.3 times.

The growth of manufacturing in Brazil was 0.4% in the 1990s, ranked 144th in the world. The growth of manufacturing in Brazil (0.39%) was less than growth of manufacturing in the world (2.0%), was less than growth of manufacturing in the Americas (3.0%).

Comparison with neighbors. The value added of manufacturing in Brazil was greater than in Argentina ($42.5 billion), in Venezuela ($15.3 billion), in Colombia ($14.7 billion), in Peru ($7.1 billion), in Uruguay ($3.0 billion), in Paraguay ($2.7 billion), and in Bolivia ($1.1 billion). The manufacturing per capita in Brazil was greater than in Paraguay ($572.4), in Colombia ($408.1), in Peru ($294.9), and in Bolivia ($139.2); but less than in Argentina ($1 228.5), in Uruguay ($925.6), and in Venezuela ($705.9). The growth of manufacturing in Brazil was greater than in Uruguay (-0.34%); but less than in Bolivia (4.1%), in Argentina (3.8%), in Peru (2.4%), in Venezuela (1.5%), in Paraguay (1.1%), and in Colombia (0.52%).

Comparison with leaders. The value of manufacturing in Brazil was less than in the USA ($1.2 trillion), in Japan ($1.0 trillion), in Germany ($468.8 billion), in Italy ($227.8 billion), and in France ($215.0 billion). The manufacturing per capita in Brazil was less than in Japan ($8.3 thousand), in Germany ($5.8 thousand), in the United States ($4.7 thousand), in Italy ($4.0 thousand), and in France ($3.6 thousand). The growth of manufacturing in Brazil was greater than in Germany (0.26%); but less than in the United States (3.2%), in France (2.4%), in Italy (1.2%), and in Japan (1.1%).

The 2000s

The manufacturing of Brazil was $135.8 billion per year in the 2000s, ranked 13th in the world, and was on a par with India ($136.8 billion). The share in the world was 1.8%, and 6.0% in the Americas.

Chapter 5.1. Manufacturing

The share of manufacturing in the economy of Brazil was 16.4% in the 2000s, ranked 65th in the world, and was on a par with Bangladesh (16.4%).

The value of manufacturing per capita in Brazil was $734.9 in the 2000s, ranked 81st in the world, and was on a par with Serbia ($732.0), South America ($728.1). The value added of manufacturing per capita in Brazil was less than manufacturing per capita in the world ($1 138.1) by 35.4%, and was less than manufacturing per capita in the Americas ($2 583.7) in 3.5 times.

The growth of manufacturing in Brazil was 2.3% in the 2000s, ranked 114th in the world, and was on a par with Eswatini (2.3%), the Maldives (2.3%). The growth of manufacturing in Brazil (2.3%) was less than growth of manufacturing in the world (4.2%), was greater than growth of manufacturing in the Americas (1.4%).

Comparison with neighbors. The value of manufacturing in Brazil was greater than in Argentina ($40.1 billion), in Venezuela ($26.0 billion), in Colombia ($23.5 billion), in Peru ($12.7 billion), in Paraguay ($3.0 billion), in Uruguay ($2.9 billion), and in Bolivia ($1.3 billion). The value added of manufacturing per capita in Brazil was greater than in Colombia ($555.2), in Paraguay ($517.9), in Peru ($457.3), and in Bolivia ($143.6); but less than in Argentina ($1 037.2), in Venezuela ($993.0), and in Uruguay ($870.9). The growth of manufacturing in Brazil was greater than in Argentina (2.2%), in Venezuela (1.5%), and in Paraguay (0.15%); but less than in Peru (5.0%), in Colombia (4.3%), in Bolivia (4.0%), and in Uruguay (3.5%).

Comparison with leaders. The value of manufacturing in Brazil was less than in the USA ($1.6 trillion), in China ($1.1 trillion), in Japan ($992.9 billion), in Germany ($551.4 billion), and in Italy ($277.2 billion). The value of manufacturing per capita in Brazil was less than in Japan ($7.7 thousand), in Germany ($6.8 thousand), in the United States ($5.6 thousand), in Italy ($4.8 thousand), and in China ($815.3). The growth of manufacturing in Brazil was greater than in the USA (1.6%), in Japan (0.32%), in Germany (0.097%), and in Italy (-1.3%).

The 2010s

The Brazilian manufacturing was $232.9 billion per year in the 2010s, ranked 10th in the world. The share in the world was 1.9%, and 7.7% in the Americas.

The share of manufacturing in the economy of Brazil was 12.6% in the 2010s, ranked 95th in the world, and was on a par with Namibia (12.6%), Northern Europe (12.6%), Ghana (12.7%).

The Brazilian manufacturing per capita was $1 144.2 in the 2010s, ranked 75th in the world, and was on a par with Kazakhstan ($1 170.2), South America ($1 170.9). The value of manufacturing per capita in Brazil was less than manufacturing per capita in the world ($1 697.4) by 32.6%, and was less than manufacturing per capita in the Americas ($3 100.6) in 2.7 times.

The growth of manufacturing in Brazil was -0.3% in the 2010s, ranked 179th in the world. The growth of manufacturing in Brazil (-0.31%) was less than growth of manufacturing in the world (3.9%), was less than growth of manufacturing in the Americas (1.6%).

Comparison with neighbors. The Brazil's manufacturing was 3.0 times higher than in Argentina ($78.9 billion), 5.7 times higher than in Venezuela ($41.0 billion), 5.7 times higher than in Colombia ($40.7 billion), 8.6 times higher than in Peru ($27.2 billion), 34.0 times higher than in Paraguay ($6.8 billion), 35.5 times higher than in Uruguay ($6.6 billion), and 70.1 times higher than in Bolivia ($3.3 billion). The sector of manufacturing per capita in Brazil was 11.1% higher than in Paraguay ($1 029.8), 28.5% higher than in Peru ($890.7), 33.4% higher than in Colombia ($857.5), and 3.7 times higher than in Bolivia ($307.8); but 40.5% lower than in Uruguay ($1 922.7), 37.9% lower than in Argentina ($1 841.2), and 18.2% lower than in Venezuela ($1 399.4). The growth of manufacturing in Brazil was greater than in Venezuela (-11.8%); but less than in Paraguay (4.4%), in Bolivia (4.4%), in Peru (2.7%), in Colombia (1.9%), in Uruguay (0.85%), and in Argentina (-0.30%).

Comparison with leaders. The value added of manufacturing in Brazil was 13.4 times lower than in China ($3.1 trillion), 8.9 times lower than in the United States ($2.1 trillion), 4.6 times lower than in Japan ($1.1 trillion), 3.2 times lower than in Germany ($735.2 billion), and 40.4% lower than in Republic of Korea ($390.5 billion). The manufacturing per capita in Brazil was 7.8 times lower than in Germany ($9.0 thousand), 7.2 times lower than in Japan ($8.3 thousand), 6.8 times lower than in Republic of Korea ($7.7 thousand), 5.7 times lower than in the USA ($6.5 thousand), and 48.5% lower than in China ($2.2 thousand). The growth of manufacturing in Brazil was less than in China (7.5%), in South Korea (3.8%), in Germany (3.5%), in Japan (3.0%), and in the United States (1.9%).

Chapter VI. Construction

(ISIC F)

The sector of construction in Brazil grew from $6.1 billion per year in the 1970s to $107.3 billion per year in the 2010s, that is by $101.2 billion or 17.6 times. The change occurred at $90.8 billion due to a 6.5-fold increase in prices, as also at $4.8 billion due to a 1.4-fold increase in productivity, as well as at $5.6 billion due to the expansion in population. The average annual growth in construction is 2.8%. The minimum value of construction was in 1970 at $1.7 billion. The maximum value of construction was in 2011 at $139.6 billion.

Chapter VI. Construction

The 1970s

The value of construction in Brazil was $6.1 billion per year in the 1970s, ranked 14th in the world, and was on a par with China ($6.1 billion). The share in the world was 1.4%, and 5.0% in the Americas.

The share of construction in the economy of Brazil was 6.3% in the 1970s, ranked 93rd in the world, and was on a par with Burkina Faso (6.2%).

The value of construction per capita in Brazil was $57.5 in the 1970s, ranked 87th in the world, and was on a par with Southern Africa ($58.8), Cabo Verde ($58.9). The value of construction per capita in Brazil was less than construction per capita in the world ($106.1) by 45.8%, and was less than construction per capita in the Americas ($217.5) in 3.8 times.

The growth of construction in Brazil was 9.3% in the 1970s, ranked 37th in the world. The growth of construction in Brazil (9.3%) was greater than growth of construction in the world (2.1%), was greater than growth of construction in the Americas (1.5%).

Comparison with neighbors. The Brazil's construction was greater than in Venezuela ($5.1 billion), in Argentina ($3.3 billion), in Colombia ($678.4 million), in Peru ($304.6 million), in Uruguay ($231.5 million), in Bolivia ($115.6 million), and in Paraguay ($61.3 million). The sector of construction per capita in Brazil was greater than in Colombia ($28.5), in Bolivia ($23.3), in Paraguay ($22.1), and in Peru ($20.0); but less than in Venezuela ($391.9), in Argentina ($127.8), and in Uruguay ($81.5). The growth of construction in Brazil was greater than in Uruguay (9.0%), in Bolivia (4.9%), in Colombia (4.2%), in Peru (3.5%), and in Argentina (2.8%); but less than in Paraguay (19.6%) and in Venezuela (11.8%).

Comparison with leaders. The Brazil's construction was less than in the USA ($81.1 billion), in the USSR ($52.5 billion), in Japan ($43.5 billion), in Germany ($33.8 billion), and in France ($22.4 billion). The value of construction per capita in Brazil was less than in Germany ($428.6), in France ($417.3), in Japan ($390.8), in the United States ($371.5), and in the USSR ($208.1). The growth of construction in Brazil was greater than in the USSR (6.5%), in Japan (3.4%), in France (2.0%), in Germany (0.66%), and in the United States (0.31%).

The 1980s

The value of construction in Brazil was $16.4 billion per year in the 1980s, ranked 11th in the world, and was on a par with Australasia ($16.3 billion), Oceania ($16.8 billion), Mexico ($16.8 billion). The share in the world was 1.8%, and 6.2% in the Americas.

The share of construction in the economy of Brazil was 6.9% in the 1980s, ranked 60th in the world, and was on a par with Chile (6.9%), Oceania (6.9%), Romania (6.9%).

The Brazilian construction per capita was $122.8 in the 1980s, ranked 80th in the world. The value of construction per capita in Brazil was less than construction per capita in the world ($186.2) by 34.0%, and was less than construction per capita in the Americas ($396.8) in 3.2 times.

The growth of construction in Brazil was 2% in the 1980s, ranked 101st in the world. The growth of construction in Brazil (2.0%) was greater than growth of construction in the world (1.7%), was greater than growth of construction in the Americas (0.83%).

Comparison with neighbors. The construction of Brazil was greater than in Venezuela ($6.9 billion), in Argentina ($5.3 billion), in Colombia ($2.5 billion), in Peru ($770.5 million), in Uruguay ($397.4 million), in Paraguay ($305.2 million), and in Bolivia ($150.2

million). The Brazil's construction per capita was greater than in Colombia ($85.6), in Paraguay ($84.0), in Peru ($39.4), and in Bolivia ($24.5); but less than in Venezuela ($405.1), in Argentina ($177.3), and in Uruguay ($132.4). The growth of construction in Brazil was greater than in Peru (0.27%), in Argentina (-4.9%), in Uruguay (-5.0%), in Bolivia (-6.8%), and in Venezuela (-9.7%); but less than in Colombia (5.0%) and in Paraguay (3.2%).

Comparison with leaders. The Brazil's construction was less than in the United States ($180.6 billion), in Japan ($138.7 billion), in the USSR ($72.1 billion), in Germany ($57.8 billion), and in France ($42.5 billion). The sector of construction per capita in Brazil was less than in Japan ($1 143.9), in the United States ($754.4), in France ($751.9), in Germany ($740.2), and in the USSR ($262.0). The growth of construction in Brazil was greater than in the United States (1.1%), in France (0.67%), and in Germany (-0.52%); but less than in the USSR (6.2%) and in Japan (2.1%).

The 1990s

The value added of construction in Brazil was $34.9 billion per year in the 1990s, ranked 10th in the world. The share in the world was 2.2%, and 8.0% in the Americas.

The share of construction in the economy of Brazil was 6.1% in the 1990s, ranked 81st in the world, and was on a par with Uruguay (6.1%), Libya (6.1%), Ireland (6.1%).

The Brazilian construction per capita was $217.4 in the 1990s, ranked 72nd in the world, and was on a par with Saint Vincent and the Grenadines ($213.8). The sector of construction per capita in Brazil was less than construction per capita in the world ($278.6) by 22.0%, and was less than construction per capita in the Americas ($564.1) in 2.6 times.

The growth of construction in Brazil was 1.3% in the 1990s, ranked 124th in the world. The growth of construction in Brazil (1.3%) was greater than growth of construction in the world (0.71%), was less than growth of construction in the Americas (1.8%).

Comparison with neighbors. The value of construction in Brazil was greater than in Argentina ($11.1 billion), in Venezuela ($5.1 billion), in Colombia ($4.9 billion), in Peru ($2.4 billion), in Uruguay ($1.1 billion), in Paraguay ($424.9 million), and in Bolivia ($208.5 million). The value added of construction per capita in Brazil was greater than in Colombia ($135.3), in Peru ($100.9), in Paraguay ($90.0), and in Bolivia ($27.6); but less than in Uruguay ($329.0), in Argentina ($321.5), and in Venezuela ($236.8). The growth of construction in Brazil was greater than in Paraguay (-0.079%) and in Colombia (-3.2%); but less than in Peru (6.9%), in Bolivia (5.9%), in Argentina (4.9%), in Uruguay (4.6%), and in Venezuela (3.4%).

Comparison with leaders. The value of construction in Brazil was less than in Japan ($343.2 billion), in the United States ($299.1 billion), in Germany ($125.2 billion), in the UK ($69.8 billion), and in France ($68.8 billion). The Brazil's construction per capita was less than in Japan ($2.7 thousand), in Germany ($1 552.3), in the United Kingdom ($1 205.1), in France ($1 158.8), and in the United States ($1 131.2). The growth of construction in Brazil was greater than in Germany (-0.047%), in the UK (-0.34%), in France (-0.65%), and in Japan (-1.0%); but less than in the United States (1.8%).

The 2000s

The value of construction in Brazil was $39.8 billion per year in the 2000s, ranked 15th in the world, and was on a par with Russia ($40.5 billion). The share in the world was 1.6%, and 4.9% in the Americas.

The share of construction in the economy of Brazil was 4.8% in the 2000s, ranked 147th in the world, and was on a par with French Polynesia (4.8%), Georgia (4.8%), Tunisia (4.8%).

The value of construction per capita in Brazil was $215.3 in the 2000s, ranked 103rd in the world, and was on a par with Turkmenistan ($213.6), Cuba ($219.4), Dominica ($210.5). The Brazilian construction per capita was less than construction per capita in the world ($381.3) by 43.5%, and was less than construction per capita in the Americas ($931.0) in 4.3 times.

The growth of construction in Brazil was 2.4% in the 2000s, ranked 144th in the world, and was on a par with Malaysia (2.4%). The growth of construction in Brazil (2.4%) was greater than growth of construction in the world (1.5%), was greater than growth of construction in the Americas (-0.96%).

Comparison with neighbors. The sector of construction in Brazil was greater than in Venezuela ($14.8 billion), in Argentina ($9.2 billion), in Colombia ($6.9 billion), in Peru ($4.1 billion), in Uruguay ($1.3 billion), in Paraguay ($600.9 million), and in Bolivia ($271.4 million). The value of construction per capita in Brazil was greater than in Colombia ($162.1), in Peru ($147.2), in Paraguay ($104.3), and in Bolivia ($29.7); but less than in Venezuela ($563.8), in Uruguay ($377.0), and in Argentina ($238.7). The growth of

Chapter VI. Construction

construction in Brazil was greater than in Paraguay (1.8%), in Argentina (1.7%), and in Uruguay (0.071%); but less than in Colombia (7.2%), in Peru (6.4%), in Venezuela (5.5%), and in Bolivia (2.6%).

Comparison with leaders. The Brazil's construction was less than in the USA ($583.0 billion), in Japan ($270.5 billion), in China ($150.1 billion), in the UK ($132.1 billion), and in Spain ($111.8 billion). The value added of construction per capita in Brazil was greater than in China ($113.1); but less than in Spain ($2.6 thousand), in the UK ($2.2 thousand), in Japan ($2.1 thousand), and in the United States ($1 983.7). The growth of construction in Brazil was greater than in Spain (1.7%), in the UK (0.17%), in the United States (-2.6%), and in Japan (-3.9%); but less than in China (11.9%).

The 2010s

The sector of construction in Brazil was $107.3 billion per year in the 2010s, ranked 11th in the world, and was on a par with Central America ($105.6 billion). The share in the world was 2.6%, and 9.3% in the Americas.

The share of construction in the economy of Brazil was 5.8% in the 2010s, ranked 115th in the world, and was on a par with Africa (5.8%), the TCI (5.8%), Iraq (5.8%).

The value added of construction per capita in Brazil was $527.4 in the 2010s, ranked 85th in the world, and was on a par with Hungary ($524.2), Suriname ($521.6), China ($521.3). The sector of construction per capita in Brazil was less than construction per capita in the world ($572.1) by 7.8%, and was less than construction per capita in the Americas ($1 189.0) in 2.3 times.

The growth of construction in Brazil was 0% in the 2010s, ranked 164th in the world. The growth of construction in Brazil (0.040%) was less than growth of construction in the world (2.9%), was less than growth of construction in the Americas (1.3%).

Comparison with neighbors. The Brazilian construction was 4.4 times higher than in Argentina ($24.6 billion), 4.4 times higher than in Venezuela ($24.2 billion), 4.9 times higher than in Colombia ($21.7 billion), 8.2 times higher than in Peru ($13.0 billion), 21.5 times higher than in Uruguay ($5.0 billion), 49.6 times higher than in Paraguay ($2.2 billion), and 118.4 times higher than in Bolivia ($906.9 million). The sector of construction per capita in Brazil was 15.4% higher than in Colombia ($457.1), 23.5% higher than in Peru ($427.0), 61.9% higher than in Paraguay ($325.8), and 6.3 times higher than in Bolivia ($84.1); but 2.8 times lower than in Uruguay ($1 464.6), 36.1% lower than in Venezuela ($825.1), and 8.0% lower than in Argentina ($573.5). The growth of construction in Brazil was greater than in Venezuela (-10.7%); but less than in Bolivia (6.5%), in Paraguay (5.2%), in Peru (4.7%), in Colombia (3.7%), in Argentina (1.1%), and in Uruguay (0.57%).

Comparison with leaders. The construction of Brazil was 6.8 times lower than in China ($731.1 billion), 6.3 times lower than in the USA ($680.8 billion), 2.6 times lower than in Japan ($278.7 billion), 36.1% lower than in India ($168.1 billion), and 29.9% lower than in Germany ($153.2 billion). The value of construction per capita in Brazil was 1.2% higher than in China ($521.3) and 4.1 times higher than in India ($129.1); but 4.1 times lower than in Japan ($2.2 thousand), 4.0 times lower than in the USA ($2.1 thousand), and 3.5 times lower than in Germany ($1 871.9). The growth of construction in Brazil was less than in China (8.2%), in India (5.2%), in Germany (1.8%), in Japan (1.7%), and in the USA (1.4%).

Chapter VII. Transportation

Transport, storage and communication (ISIC I)

The Brazilian transportation rose from $4.4 billion per year in the 1970s to $146.6 billion per year in the 2010s, that is by $142.2 billion or 33.3 times. The change occurred at $127.7 billion due to a 7.8-fold increase in prices, as also at $10.5 billion due to a 2.2-fold increase in productivity, as well as at $4.0 billion due to the growing in population. The average annual growth in transportation is 4.1%. The minimum value of transportation was in 1970 at $1.4 billion. The maximum value of transportation was in 2011 at $180.9 billion.

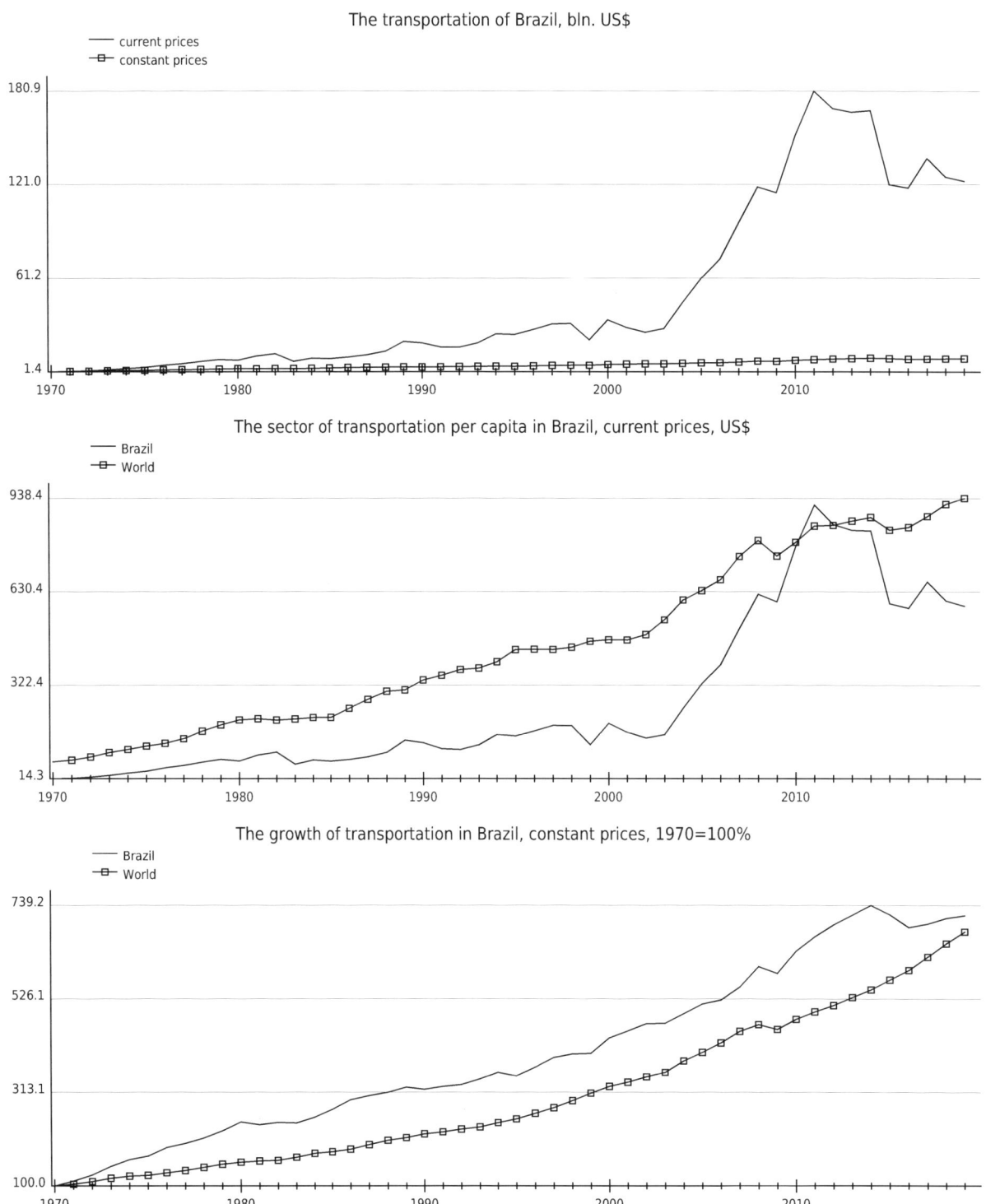

Chapter VII. Transportation

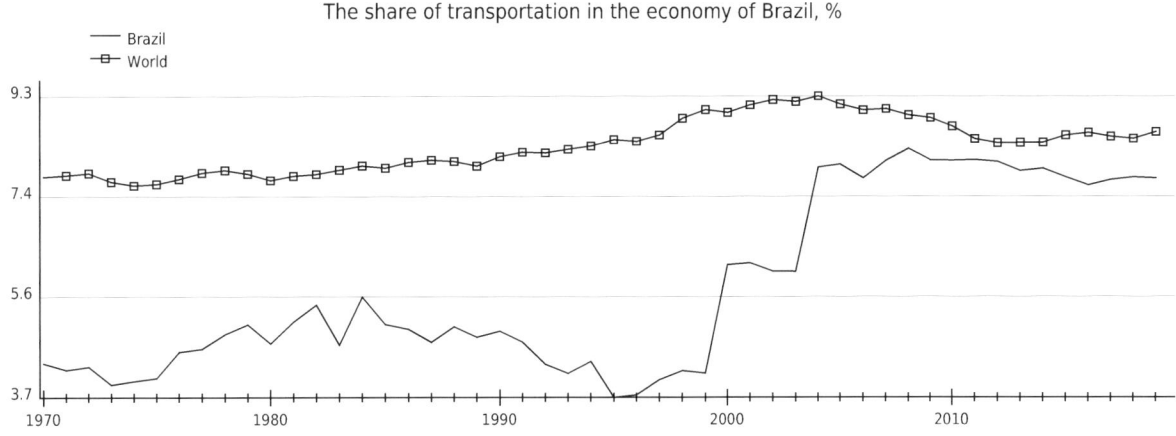

The 1970s

The value added of transportation in Brazil was $4.4 billion per year in the 1970s, ranked 18th in the world. The share in the world was 0.89%, and 2.2% in the Americas.

The share of transportation in the economy of Brazil was 4.5% in the 1970s, ranked 142nd in the world, and was on a par with Dominica (4.5%), Algeria (4.5%), Guinea (4.5%).

The transportation per capita in Brazil was $41.4 in the 1970s, ranked 114th in the world, and was on a par with Guyana ($40.8), Belize ($42.2). The value added of transportation per capita in Brazil was less than transportation per capita in the world ($122.3) in 3.0 times, and was less than transportation per capita in the Americas ($360.9) in 8.7 times.

The growth of transportation in Brazil was 9.4% in the 1970s, ranked 26th in the world, and was on a par with Turkey (9.4%). The growth of transportation in Brazil (9.4%) was greater than growth of transportation in the world (4.6%), was greater than growth of transportation in the Americas (4.9%).

Comparison with neighbors. The Brazil's transportation was greater than in Argentina ($1.8 billion), in Colombia ($1.3 billion), in Venezuela ($1.1 billion), in Peru ($1.0 billion), in Uruguay ($229.8 million), in Bolivia ($141.9 million), and in Paraguay ($110.1 million). The transportation per capita in Brazil was greater than in Paraguay ($39.8) and in Bolivia ($28.6); but less than in Venezuela ($82.2), in Uruguay ($80.9), in Argentina ($70.0), in Peru ($67.4), and in Colombia ($55.1). The growth of transportation in Brazil was greater than in Colombia (7.8%), in Venezuela (7.3%), in Uruguay (2.7%), in Peru (2.5%), and in Argentina (2.0%); but less than in Bolivia (11.3%) and in Paraguay (9.6%).

Comparison with leaders. The value of transportation in Brazil was less than in the United States ($168.6 billion), in Japan ($46.4 billion), in Germany ($29.6 billion), in the USSR ($28.8 billion), and in France ($24.0 billion). The value added of transportation per capita in Brazil was less than in the USA ($772.4), in France ($447.4), in Japan ($416.6), in Germany ($376.1), and in the USSR ($114.0). The growth of transportation in Brazil was greater than in the USSR (8.1%), in the USA (4.2%), in France (4.1%), in Germany (3.0%), and in Japan (1.7%).

The 1980s

The value added of transportation in Brazil was $11.8 billion per year in the 1980s, ranked 17th in the world. The share in the world was 1.0%, and 2.5% in the Americas.

The share of transportation in the economy of Brazil was 5.0% in the 1980s, ranked 140th in the world, and was on a par with India (5.0%).

The Brazilian transportation per capita was $88.6 in the 1980s, ranked 108th in the world, and was on a par with Nicaragua ($88.1), Micronesia ($89.7), Asia ($86.8). The sector of transportation per capita in Brazil was less than transportation per capita in the world ($242.0) in 2.7 times, and was less than transportation per capita in the Americas ($714.8) in 8.1 times.

The growth of transportation in Brazil was 3.7% in the 1980s, ranked 93rd in the world, and was on a par with Jamaica (3.7%), Senegal (3.7%). The growth of transportation in Brazil (3.7%) was greater than growth of transportation in the world (3.4%), was greater than growth of transportation in the Americas (3.5%).

Comparison with neighbors. The transportation of Brazil was greater than in Colombia ($3.3 billion), in Argentina ($3.0 billion), in Venezuela ($2.4 billion), in Peru ($2.1 billion), in Uruguay ($433.2 million), in Paraguay ($392.6 million), and in Bolivia ($319.0 million). The value added of transportation per capita in Brazil was greater than in Bolivia ($52.0); but less than in Uruguay ($144.3), in Venezuela ($137.8), in Colombia ($112.0), in Paraguay ($108.1), in Peru ($106.8), and in Argentina ($99.6). The growth of transportation in Brazil was greater than in Bolivia (3.4%), in Colombia (2.7%), in Uruguay (2.2%), in Argentina (1.3%), in Peru (0.83%), and in Venezuela (0.66%); but less than in Paraguay (4.4%).

Comparison with leaders. The transportation of Brazil was less than in the USA ($394.9 billion), in Japan ($147.7 billion), in Germany ($56.6 billion), in France ($56.2 billion), and in the UK ($53.0 billion). The value of transportation per capita in Brazil was less than in the USA ($1 649.2), in Japan ($1 217.8), in France ($993.7), in the UK ($938.7), and in Germany ($725.5). The growth of transportation in Brazil was greater than in the USA (3.6%), in the United Kingdom (3.0%), and in Germany (1.8%); but less than in France (5.4%) and in Japan (4.7%).

The 1990s

The sector of transportation in Brazil was $23.8 billion per year in the 1990s, ranked 17th in the world. The share in the world was 1.0%, and 2.8% in the Americas.

The share of transportation in the economy of Brazil was 4.1% in the 1990s, ranked 185th in the world, and was on a par with Tajikistan (4.1%), Palestine (4.1%), Myanmar (4.1%).

The value of transportation per capita in Brazil was $148.0 in the 1990s, ranked 104th in the world, and was on a par with Djibouti ($148.8), Belarus ($150.4), Kazakhstan ($151.2). The sector of transportation per capita in Brazil was less than transportation per capita in the world ($409.5) in 2.8 times, and was less than transportation per capita in the Americas ($1 104.4) in 7.5 times.

The growth of transportation in Brazil was 2.2% in the 1990s, ranked 151st in the world. The growth of transportation in Brazil (2.2%) was less than growth of transportation in the world (4.0%), was less than growth of transportation in the Americas (4.7%).

Comparison with neighbors. The Brazilian transportation was greater than in Argentina ($13.8 billion), in Colombia ($7.0 billion), in Venezuela ($3.8 billion), in Peru ($3.7 billion), in Uruguay ($1.3 billion), in Bolivia ($716.2 million), and in Paraguay ($603.4 million). The value of transportation per capita in Brazil was greater than in Paraguay ($127.8) and in Bolivia ($94.9); but less than in Uruguay ($405.1), in Argentina ($399.1), in Colombia ($192.7), in Venezuela ($177.4), and in Peru ($153.2). The growth of transportation in Brazil was greater than in Venezuela (1.3%); but less than in Uruguay (9.0%), in Argentina (6.2%), in Bolivia (5.5%), in Paraguay (5.3%), in Colombia (3.6%), and in Peru (3.0%).

Comparison with leaders. The transportation of Brazil was less than in the USA ($702.6 billion), in Japan ($373.9 billion), in Germany ($144.3 billion), in France ($118.7 billion), and in the United Kingdom ($117.6 billion). The sector of transportation per capita in Brazil was less than in Japan ($3.0 thousand), in the United States ($2.7 thousand), in the United Kingdom ($2.0 thousand), in France ($1 999.2), and in Germany ($1 789.0). The growth of transportation in Brazil was less than in the USA (5.0%), in France (4.8%), in the UK (4.7%), in Germany (3.9%), and in Japan (3.0%).

The 2000s

The transportation of Brazil was $63.1 billion per year in the 2000s, ranked 13th in the world. The share in the world was 1.6%, and 4.3% in the Americas.

The share of transportation in the economy of Brazil was 7.6% in the 2000s, ranked 138th in the world, and was on a par with Canada (7.6%), Benin (7.7%), the Bahamas (7.6%).

The transportation per capita in Brazil was $341.6 in the 2000s, ranked 100th in the world, and was on a par with South America ($340.1), Gabon ($337.7), Cuba ($337.1). The Brazilian transportation per capita was less than transportation per capita in the world ($621.1) by 45.0%, and was less than transportation per capita in the Americas ($1 687.7) in 4.9 times.

The growth of transportation in Brazil was 3.8% in the 2000s, ranked 134th in the world, and was on a par with Australasia (3.8%). The growth of transportation in Brazil (3.8%) was less than growth of transportation in the world (3.9%), was greater than growth of transportation in the Americas (3.2%).

Comparison with neighbors. The value of transportation in Brazil was greater than in Argentina ($15.0 billion), in Colombia ($12.3 billion), in Venezuela ($10.6 billion), in Peru ($6.1 billion), in Uruguay ($1.6 billion), in Bolivia ($1.1 billion), and in Paraguay ($1.0

Chapter VII. Transportation

billion). The value added of transportation per capita in Brazil was greater than in Colombia ($290.5), in Peru ($221.1), in Paraguay ($181.3), and in Bolivia ($123.2); but less than in Uruguay ($493.5), in Venezuela ($404.7), and in Argentina ($387.4). The growth of transportation in Brazil was greater than in Bolivia (3.7%); but less than in Venezuela (8.5%), in Uruguay (7.9%), in Argentina (5.3%), in Paraguay (5.0%), in Colombia (4.5%), and in Peru (4.4%).

Comparison with leaders. The value of transportation in Brazil was less than in the USA ($1.2 trillion), in Japan ($468.5 billion), in Germany ($228.2 billion), in the UK ($215.9 billion), and in France ($185.6 billion). The sector of transportation per capita in Brazil was less than in the United States ($4.0 thousand), in Japan ($3.7 thousand), in the United Kingdom ($3.6 thousand), in France ($3.0 thousand), and in Germany ($2.8 thousand). The growth of transportation in Brazil was greater than in Germany (3.4%), in the UK (3.1%), in the United States (3.1%), in France (2.7%), and in Japan (1.5%).

The 2010s

The sector of transportation in Brazil was $146.6 billion per year in the 2010s, ranked 8th in the world. The share in the world was 2.3%, and 6.3% in the Americas.

The share of transportation in the economy of Brazil was 7.9% in the 2010s, ranked 133rd in the world, and was on a par with Southern Asia (7.9%), New Zealand (7.8%), Nepal (8.0%).

The transportation per capita in Brazil was $720.2 in the 2010s, ranked 92nd in the world, and was on a par with Argentina ($729.0), Eastern Asia ($710.0), Equatorial Guinea ($737.5). The value of transportation per capita in Brazil was less than transportation per capita in the world ($864.8) by 16.7%, and was less than transportation per capita in the Americas ($2 381.9) in 3.3 times.

The growth of transportation in Brazil was 2.1% in the 2010s, ranked 161st in the world, and was on a par with Australia (2.1%), Southern Africa (2.1%). The growth of transportation in Brazil (2.1%) was less than growth of transportation in the world (4.0%), was less than growth of transportation in the Americas (4.7%).

Comparison with neighbors. The sector of transportation in Brazil was 4.7 times higher than in Argentina ($31.2 billion), 5.8 times higher than in Colombia ($25.3 billion), 9.0 times higher than in Venezuela ($16.2 billion), 9.2 times higher than in Peru ($16.0 billion), 46.6 times higher than in Uruguay ($3.1 billion), 52.0 times higher than in Bolivia ($2.8 billion), and 56.8 times higher than in Paraguay ($2.6 billion). The transportation per capita in Brazil was 30.4% higher than in Venezuela ($552.4), 35.0% higher than in Colombia ($533.3), 37.2% higher than in Peru ($525.0), 85.4% higher than in Paraguay ($388.5), and 2.8 times higher than in Bolivia ($261.3); but 22.0% lower than in Uruguay ($923.3) and 1.2% lower than in Argentina ($729.0). The growth of transportation in Brazil was greater than in Venezuela (-8.7%); but less than in Uruguay (8.2%), in Peru (7.2%), in Bolivia (5.1%), in Paraguay (5.0%), in Colombia (4.0%), and in Argentina (2.3%).

Comparison with leaders. The value of transportation in Brazil was 12.2 times lower than in the USA ($1.8 trillion), 3.6 times lower than in Japan ($529.8 billion), 3.2 times lower than in China ($464.2 billion), 2.0 times lower than in Germany ($300.0 billion), and 43.1% lower than in the United Kingdom ($257.7 billion). The value of transportation per capita in Brazil was 2.2 times higher than in China ($331.0); but 7.8 times lower than in the United States ($5.6 thousand), 5.8 times lower than in Japan ($4.1 thousand), 5.5 times lower than in the United Kingdom ($3.9 thousand), and 5.1 times lower than in Germany ($3.7 thousand). The growth of transportation in Brazil was greater than in Japan (0.81%); but less than in China (7.5%), in the USA (5.1%), in the United Kingdom (2.8%), and in Germany (2.7%).

Chapter VIII. Trade

Wholesale, retail trade, restaurants and hotels (ISIC G-H)

The sector of trade in Brazil enlarged from $13.0 billion per year in the 1970s to $287.2 billion per year in the 2010s, that is by $274.1 billion or 22.0 times. The change occurred at $238.6 billion due to a 5.9-fold increase in prices, as also at $23.6 billion due to a 1.9-fold increase in productivity, as well as at $12.0 billion due to the increase in population. The average annual growth in trade is 3.7%. The minimum value of trade was in 1970 at $5.2 billion. The maximum value of trade was in 2014 at $340.6 billion.

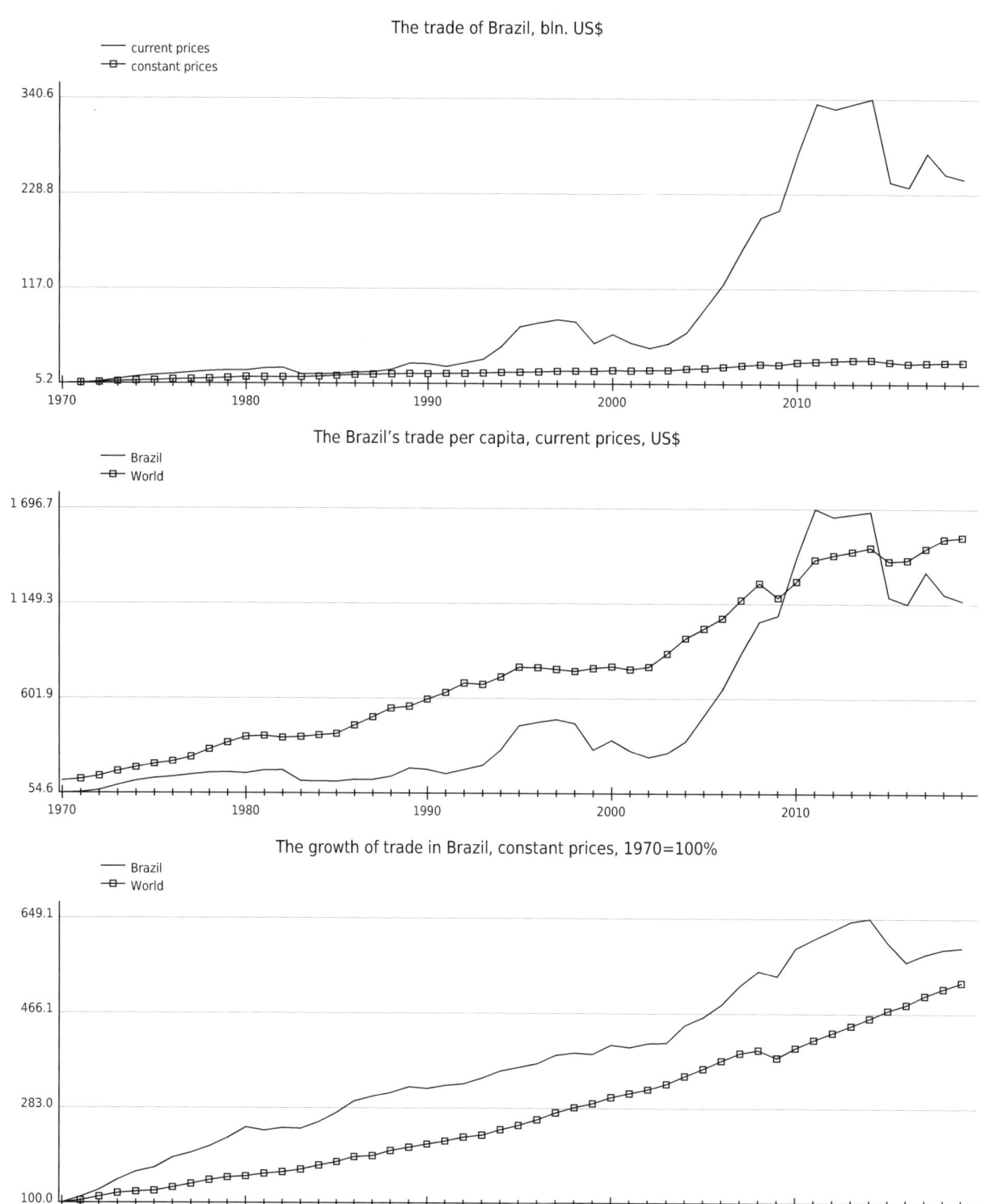

Chapter VIII. Trade

The 1970s

The value added of trade in Brazil was $13.0 billion per year in the 1970s, ranked 11th in the world, and was on a par with Oceania ($12.7 billion). The share in the world was 1.5%, and 3.6% in the Americas.

The share of trade in the economy of Brazil was 13.4% in the 1970s, ranked 109th in the world, and was on a par with Paraguay (13.4%), Southern Africa (13.4%), South Africa (13.4%).

The sector of trade per capita in Brazil was $122.9 in the 1970s, ranked 95th in the world, and was on a par with Nicaragua ($122.8), Oman ($120.4). The value added of trade per capita in Brazil was less than trade per capita in the world ($221.0) by 44.4%, and was less than trade per capita in the Americas ($654.8) in 5.3 times.

The growth of trade in Brazil was 9.4% in the 1970s, ranked 18th in the world, and was on a par with the Cayman Islands (9.4%), Egypt (9.4%). The growth of trade in Brazil (9.4%) was greater than growth of trade in the world (4.5%), was greater than growth of trade in the Americas (4.4%).

Comparison with neighbors. The trade of Brazil was greater than in Argentina ($8.2 billion), in Colombia ($2.6 billion), in Venezuela ($2.5 billion), in Peru ($1.8 billion), in Uruguay ($517.6 million), in Bolivia ($246.2 million), and in Paraguay ($244.9 million). The value added of trade per capita in Brazil was greater than in Peru ($116.8), in Colombia ($108.7), in Paraguay ($88.4), and in Bolivia ($49.7); but less than in Argentina ($318.8), in Venezuela ($191.9), and in Uruguay ($182.3). The growth of trade in Brazil was greater than in Paraguay (8.8%), in Colombia (6.1%), in Venezuela (4.7%), in Bolivia (3.5%), in Uruguay (2.8%), in Argentina (2.6%), and in Peru (2.5%).

Comparison with leaders. The value added of trade in Brazil was less than in the United States ($278.3 billion), in Japan ($90.3 billion), in the USSR ($62.3 billion), in Germany ($61.1 billion), and in France ($40.9 billion). The Brazil's trade per capita was less than in the United States ($1 275.1), in Japan ($811.1), in Germany ($775.5), in France ($762.4), and in the USSR ($247.1). The growth of trade in Brazil was greater than in Japan (8.2%), in the USSR (5.2%), in France (3.9%), in the United States (3.9%), and in Germany (3.0%).

The 1980s

The value added of trade in Brazil was $20.3 billion per year in the 1980s, ranked 15th in the world. The share in the world was 0.96%, and 2.4% in the Americas.

The share of trade in the economy of Brazil was 8.5% in the 1980s, ranked 165th in the world.

The Brazilian trade per capita was $151.8 in the 1980s, ranked 115th in the world, and was on a par with Western Africa ($151.9), Iraq ($152.2), Namibia ($149.1). The value added of trade per capita in Brazil was less than trade per capita in the world ($437.7) in 2.9 times, and was less than trade per capita in the Americas ($1 268.0) in 8.4 times.

The growth of trade in Brazil was 3.7% in the 1980s, ranked 60th in the world, and was on a par with Polynesia (3.7%). The growth of trade in Brazil (3.7%) was greater than growth of trade in the world (3.3%), was greater than growth of trade in the Americas (3.5%).

Comparison with neighbors. The Brazilian trade was greater than in Argentina ($17.1 billion), in Colombia ($6.9 billion), in Venezuela ($5.8 billion), in Peru ($4.8 billion), in Uruguay ($936.1 million), in Paraguay ($884.3 million), and in Bolivia ($518.3 million). The Brazilian trade per capita was greater than in Bolivia ($84.5); but less than in Argentina ($571.3), in Venezuela ($336.2), in Uruguay

($311.8), in Peru ($245.8), in Paraguay ($243.4), and in Colombia ($233.4). The growth of trade in Brazil was greater than in Paraguay (3.5%), in Colombia (2.4%), in Bolivia (1.8%), in Peru (0.83%), in Uruguay (0.30%), in Argentina (-1.5%), and in Venezuela (-2.0%).

Comparison with leaders. The value of trade in Brazil was less than in the USA ($653.3 billion), in Japan ($277.3 billion), in Germany ($116.7 billion), in the USSR ($112.3 billion), and in Italy ($95.7 billion). The Brazilian trade per capita was less than in the United States ($2.7 thousand), in Japan ($2.3 thousand), in Italy ($1 684.2), in Germany ($1 496.0), and in the USSR ($408.1). The growth of trade in Brazil was greater than in Italy (2.3%), in Germany (1.8%), and in the USSR (-0.62%); but less than in Japan (4.9%) and in the United States (4.4%).

The 1990s

The sector of trade in Brazil was $52.5 billion per year in the 1990s, ranked 12th in the world, and was on a par with Australasia ($52.5 billion), the Netherlands ($52.4 billion). The share in the world was 1.3%, and 3.5% in the Americas.

The share of trade in the economy of Brazil was 9.1% in the 1990s, ranked 182nd in the world, and was on a par with Bahrain (9.1%).

The sector of trade per capita in Brazil was $326.8 in the 1990s, ranked 99th in the world, and was on a par with Melanesia ($327.4), Iran ($327.8), Lithuania ($321.3). The value added of trade per capita in Brazil was less than trade per capita in the world ($721.8) in 2.2 times, and was less than trade per capita in the Americas ($1 943.2) in 5.9 times.

The growth of trade in Brazil was 1.8% in the 1990s, ranked 136th in the world, and was on a par with Bahrain (1.8%), South Africa (1.8%). The growth of trade in Brazil (1.8%) was less than growth of trade in the world (3.5%), was less than growth of trade in the Americas (3.8%).

Comparison with neighbors. The Brazil's trade was greater than in Argentina ($45.9 billion), in Colombia ($12.8 billion), in Peru ($8.7 billion), in Venezuela ($7.3 billion), in Uruguay ($2.7 billion), in Paraguay ($1.4 billion), and in Bolivia ($749.2 million). The value of trade per capita in Brazil was greater than in Paraguay ($297.9) and in Bolivia ($99.2); but less than in Argentina ($1 327.1), in Uruguay ($850.4), in Peru ($359.4), in Colombia ($355.4), and in Venezuela ($336.0). The growth of trade in Brazil was greater than in Paraguay (1.4%), in Colombia (0.062%), and in Venezuela (-0.044%); but less than in Uruguay (5.5%), in Argentina (4.5%), in Bolivia (3.5%), and in Peru (3.0%).

Comparison with leaders. The trade of Brazil was less than in the United States ($1.2 trillion), in Japan ($713.2 billion), in Germany ($243.7 billion), in Italy ($185.6 billion), and in France ($177.0 billion). The sector of trade per capita in Brazil was less than in Japan ($5.7 thousand), in the United States ($4.4 thousand), in Italy ($3.3 thousand), in Germany ($3.0 thousand), and in France ($3.0 thousand). The growth of trade in Brazil was less than in the United States (4.3%), in Japan (3.8%), in Germany (2.5%), in France (2.4%), and in Italy (1.9%).

The 2000s

The sector of trade in Brazil was $107.1 billion per year in the 2000s, ranked 12th in the world. The share in the world was 1.7%, and 4.4% in the Americas.

The share of trade in the economy of Brazil was 12.9% in the 2000s, ranked 146th in the world, and was on a par with Venezuela (12.9%), Mali (12.9%), Mongolia (13.0%).

The sector of trade per capita in Brazil was $579.6 in the 2000s, ranked 99th in the world, and was on a par with South America ($585.4), South Africa ($586.4), Botswana ($588.5). The value of trade per capita in Brazil was less than trade per capita in the world ($990.3) by 41.5%, and was less than trade per capita in the Americas ($2 770.2) in 4.8 times.

The growth of trade in Brazil was 3.3% in the 2000s, ranked 115th in the world, and was on a par with Peru (3.3%), Norway (3.3%), Liechtenstein (3.4%). The growth of trade in Brazil (3.3%) was greater than growth of trade in the world (2.7%), was greater than growth of trade in the Americas (1.6%).

Comparison with neighbors. The value of trade in Brazil was greater than in Argentina ($35.8 billion), in Venezuela ($21.3 billion), in Colombia ($17.5 billion), in Peru ($11.5 billion), in Uruguay ($2.7 billion), in Paraguay ($1.8 billion), and in Bolivia ($1.1 billion). The sector of trade per capita in Brazil was greater than in Peru ($414.3), in Colombia ($413.9), in Paraguay ($320.7), and in Bolivia ($115.6); but less than in Argentina ($925.8), in Uruguay ($816.1), and in Venezuela ($814.8). The growth of trade in Brazil was greater than in Peru (3.3%), in Bolivia (3.1%), in Paraguay (2.3%), in Argentina (2.2%), and in Uruguay (0.56%); but less than in

Chapter VIII. Trade

Venezuela (5.7%) and in Colombia (5.2%).

Comparison with leaders. The value of trade in Brazil was less than in the United States ($1.9 trillion), in Japan ($771.8 billion), in Germany ($296.0 billion), in the UK ($293.5 billion), and in China ($262.0 billion). The Brazilian trade per capita was greater than in China ($197.5); but less than in the USA ($6.4 thousand), in Japan ($6.0 thousand), in the UK ($4.9 thousand), and in Germany ($3.6 thousand). The growth of trade in Brazil was greater than in Germany (1.7%), in the United Kingdom (1.3%), in the USA (1.1%), and in Japan (-0.77%); but less than in China (11.9%).

The 2010s

The sector of trade in Brazil was $287.2 billion per year in the 2010s, ranked 7th in the world, and was on a par with Italy ($282.2 billion). The share in the world was 2.7%, and 7.7% in the Americas.

The share of trade in the economy of Brazil was 15.5% in the 2010s, ranked 106th in the world, and was on a par with Africa (15.5%), Senegal (15.6%), Malta (15.6%).

The Brazil's trade per capita was $1 411.1 in the 2010s, ranked 87th in the world, and was on a par with Montenegro ($1 403.5), Western Asia ($1 402.8), Hungary ($1 435.0). The Brazilian trade per capita was less than trade per capita in the world ($1 436.8) by 1.8%, and was less than trade per capita in the Americas ($3 802.7) in 2.7 times.

The growth of trade in Brazil was 1% in the 2010s, ranked 176th in the world. The growth of trade in Brazil (0.98%) was less than growth of trade in the world (3.3%), was less than growth of trade in the Americas (2.1%).

Comparison with neighbors. The value of trade in Brazil was 3.5 times higher than in Argentina ($82.0 billion), 5.0 times higher than in Venezuela ($57.7 billion), 7.4 times higher than in Colombia ($38.6 billion), 9.9 times higher than in Peru ($29.0 billion), 39.5 times higher than in Uruguay ($7.3 billion), 60.1 times higher than in Paraguay ($4.8 billion), and 98.2 times higher than in Bolivia ($2.9 billion). The sector of trade per capita in Brazil was 48.6% higher than in Peru ($949.8), 73.6% higher than in Colombia ($812.9), 96.3% higher than in Paraguay ($718.8), and 5.2 times higher than in Bolivia ($271.2); but 33.8% lower than in Uruguay ($2.1 thousand), 28.3% lower than in Venezuela ($1 968.1), and 26.3% lower than in Argentina ($1 913.5). The growth of trade in Brazil was greater than in Argentina (0.62%) and in Venezuela (-12.1%); but less than in Peru (5.0%), in Colombia (4.2%), in Bolivia (4.1%), in Paraguay (3.8%), and in Uruguay (2.6%).

Comparison with leaders. The Brazil's trade was 9.1 times lower than in the United States ($2.6 trillion), 4.2 times lower than in China ($1.2 trillion), 3.0 times lower than in Japan ($869.5 billion), 22.9% lower than in Germany ($372.6 billion), and 13.0% lower than in the United Kingdom ($330.0 billion). The sector of trade per capita in Brazil was 65.7% higher than in China ($851.7); but 5.8 times lower than in the United States ($8.2 thousand), 4.8 times lower than in Japan ($6.8 thousand), 3.6 times lower than in the UK ($5.0 thousand), and 3.2 times lower than in Germany ($4.6 thousand). The growth of trade in Brazil was greater than in Japan (0.77%); but less than in China (8.9%), in the UK (2.8%), in the United States (2.3%), and in Germany (2.0%).

Chapter IX. Services

(ISIC J-P)

The services of Brazil increased from $30.9 billion per year in the 1970s to $879.0 billion per year in the 2010s, that is by $848.1 billion or 28.5 times. The change occurred at $765.7 billion due to a 7.8-fold increase in prices, as also at $54.2 billion due to a 1.9-fold increase in productivity, as well as at $28.3 billion due to the growth in population. The average annual growth in services is 3.8%. The minimum value of services was in 1970 at $10.1 billion. The maximum value of services was in 2014 at $995.3 billion.

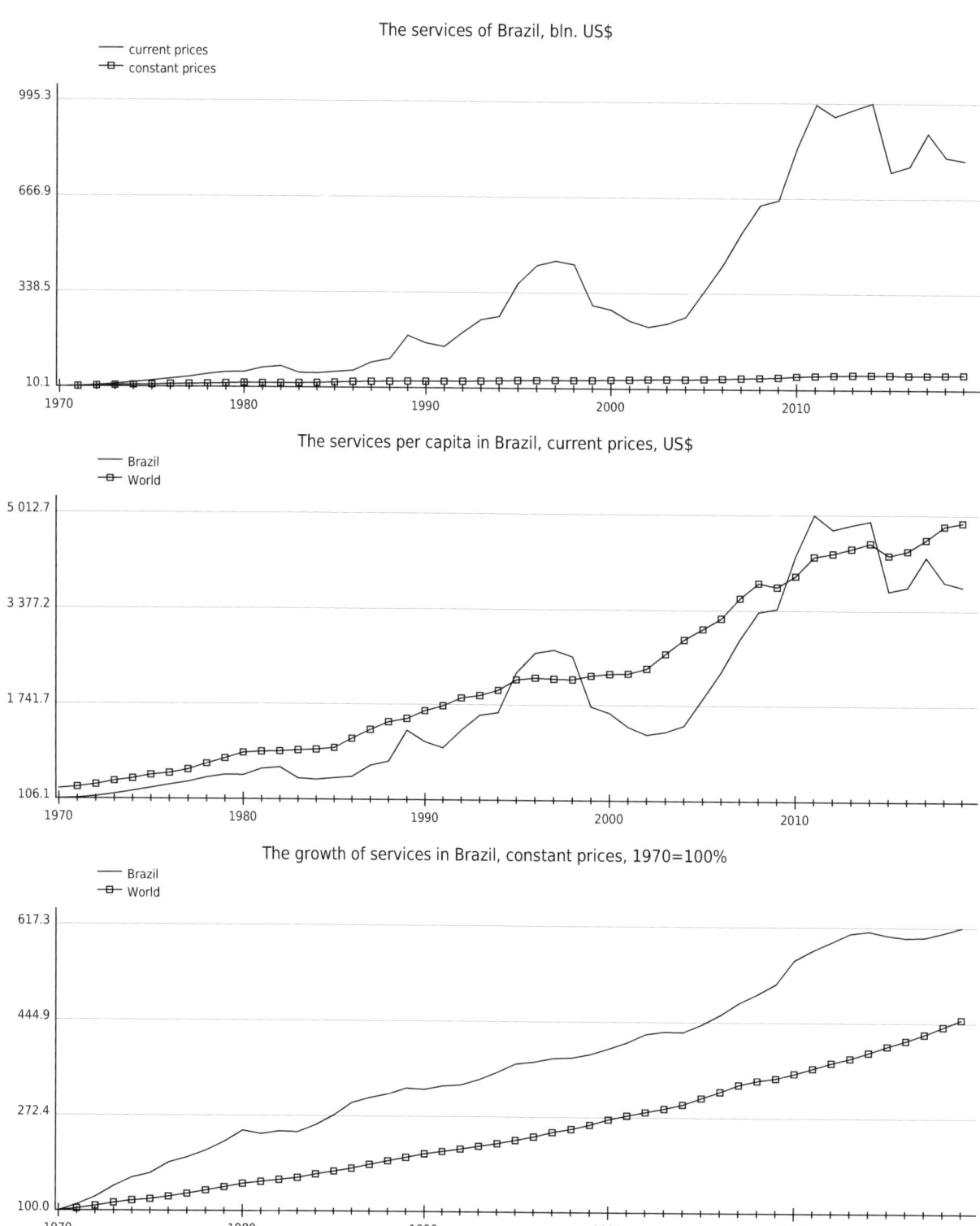

Chapter IX. Services

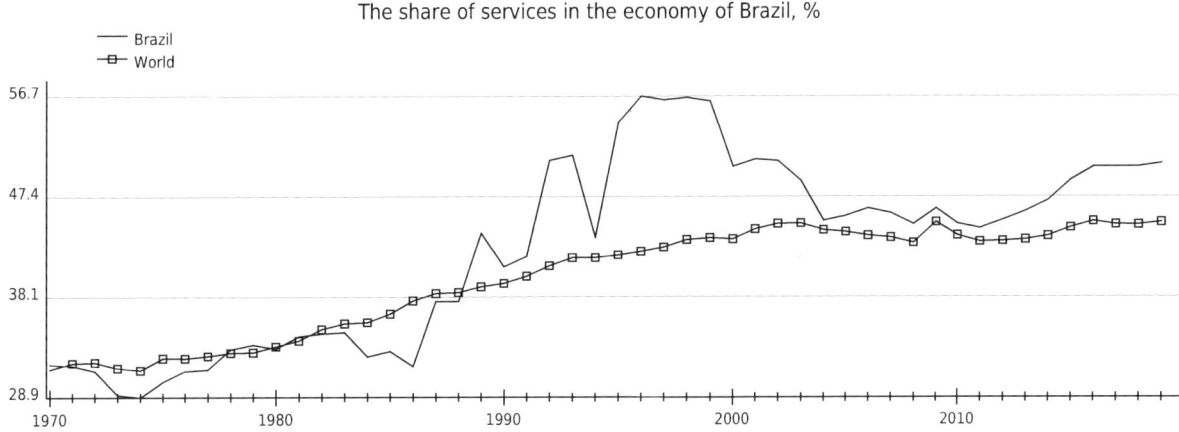

The 1970s

The value of services in Brazil was $30.9 billion per year in the 1970s, ranked 11th in the world. The share in the world was 1.5%, and 3.7% in the Americas.

The share of services in the economy of Brazil was 31.7% in the 1970s, ranked 66th in the world, and was on a par with Luxembourg (31.7%), Senegal (31.9%), Vanuatu (31.9%).

The Brazilian services per capita were $290.9 in the 1970s, ranked 85th in the world, and were on a par with Yugoslavia ($288.9), Jordan ($286.3), the Cook Islands ($284.5). The sector of services per capita in Brazil was less than services per capita in the world ($506.9) by 42.6%, and was less than services per capita in the Americas ($1 502.8) in 5.2 times.

The growth of services in Brazil was 9.4% in the 1970s, ranked 19th in the world, and was on a par with Swaziland (9.4%), the Cayman Islands (9.4%), Malaysia (9.5%). The growth of services in Brazil (9.4%) was greater than growth of services in the world (4.1%), was greater than growth of services in the Americas (3.7%).

Comparison with neighbors. The Brazilian services were greater than in Argentina ($12.4 billion), in Venezuela ($8.2 billion), in Colombia ($7.2 billion), in Peru ($1.9 billion), in Uruguay ($1.1 billion), in Bolivia ($567.1 million), and in Paraguay ($512.5 million). The services per capita in Brazil were greater than in Paraguay ($185.1), in Peru ($121.5), and in Bolivia ($114.4); but less than in Venezuela ($631.6), in Argentina ($482.7), in Uruguay ($389.2), and in Colombia ($302.2). The growth of services in Brazil was greater than in Venezuela (8.3%), in Paraguay (6.7%), in Colombia (5.9%), in Bolivia (5.8%), in Argentina (3.0%), in Peru (2.8%), and in Uruguay (1.8%).

Comparison with leaders. The value added of services in Brazil was less than in the USA ($674.4 billion), in the USSR ($168.3 billion), in Japan ($153.8 billion), in Germany ($150.2 billion), and in France ($121.8 billion). The sector of services per capita in Brazil was less than in the USA ($3.1 thousand), in France ($2.3 thousand), in Germany ($1 907.6), in Japan ($1 381.3), and in the USSR ($667.3). The growth of services in Brazil was greater than in Japan (5.9%), in Germany (4.8%), in France (3.9%), in the United States (3.3%), and in the USSR (0.90%).

The 1980s

The Brazil's services were $86.8 billion per year in the 1980s, ranked 9th in the world. The share in the world was 1.6%, and 3.8% in the Americas.

The share of services in the economy of Brazil was 36.4% in the 1980s, ranked 55th in the world, and was on a par with Saint Lucia (36.5%), Guatemala (36.3%), Montserrat (36.3%).

The sector of services per capita in Brazil was $649.3 in the 1980s, ranked 81st in the world, and was on a par with Southern Africa ($651.1), Namibia ($641.4), the Marshall Islands ($662.8). The value added of services per capita in Brazil was less than services per capita in the world ($1 115.5) by 41.8%, and was less than services per capita in the Americas ($3 456.8) in 5.3 times.

The growth of services in Brazil was 3.7% in the 1980s, ranked 87th in the world, and was on a par with Mauritius (3.7%), the Solomon Islands (3.7%). The growth of services in Brazil (3.7%) was greater than growth of services in the world (3.3%), was greater than growth of services in the Americas (2.8%).

Comparison with neighbors. The sector of services in Brazil was greater than in Argentina ($30.6 billion), in Venezuela ($18.1 billion), in Colombia ($18.0 billion), in Peru ($5.1 billion), in Uruguay ($2.8 billion), in Paraguay ($1.9 billion), and in Bolivia ($1.0 billion). The services per capita in Brazil were greater than in Colombia ($605.6), in Paraguay ($512.9), in Peru ($262.7), and in Bolivia ($168.7); but less than in Venezuela ($1 057.4), in Argentina ($1 020.8), and in Uruguay ($924.7). The growth of services in Brazil was greater than in Colombia (3.5%), in Paraguay (3.0%), in Uruguay (2.5%), in Venezuela (1.9%), in Peru (0.93%), in Argentina (0.88%), and in Bolivia (-1.6%).

Comparison with leaders. The value of services in Brazil was less than in the United States ($1.9 trillion), in Japan ($619.9 billion), in Germany ($362.2 billion), in France ($294.5 billion), and in the UK ($265.4 billion). The sector of services per capita in Brazil was less than in the USA ($7.8 thousand), in France ($5.2 thousand), in Japan ($5.1 thousand), in the UK ($4.7 thousand), and in Germany ($4.6 thousand). The growth of services in Brazil was greater than in the United Kingdom (3.3%), in Germany (3.1%), in the United States (2.8%), and in France (2.3%); but less than in Japan (4.8%).

The 1990s

The value of services in Brazil was $300.1 billion per year in the 1990s, ranked 7th in the world. The share in the world was 2.6%, and 6.3% in the Americas.

The share of services in the economy of Brazil was 52.1% in the 1990s, ranked 9th in the world, and was on a par with the Marshall Islands (52.3%).

The value added of services per capita in Brazil was $1 867.2 in the 1990s, ranked 64th in the world. The services per capita in Brazil were less than services per capita in the world ($2 014.6) by 7.3%, and were less than services per capita in the Americas ($6 173.1) in 3.3 times.

The growth of services in Brazil was 1.8% in the 1990s, ranked 146th in the world. The growth of services in Brazil (1.8%) was less than growth of services in the world (2.7%), was less than growth of services in the Americas (2.4%).

Comparison with neighbors. The sector of services in Brazil was greater than in Argentina ($99.5 billion), in Colombia ($33.4 billion), in Venezuela ($19.3 billion), in Peru ($12.3 billion), in Uruguay ($7.5 billion), in Paraguay ($2.6 billion), and in Bolivia ($1.8 billion). The value of services per capita in Brazil was greater than in Colombia ($926.6), in Venezuela ($891.8), in Paraguay ($551.6), in Peru ($509.5), and in Bolivia ($237.1); but less than in Argentina ($2.9 thousand) and in Uruguay ($2.3 thousand). The growth of services in Brazil was greater than in Venezuela (1.1%); but less than in Colombia (5.1%), in Bolivia (5.0%), in Argentina (4.1%), in Peru (2.8%), in Paraguay (2.8%), and in Uruguay (1.9%).

Comparison with leaders. The sector of services in Brazil was less than in the United States ($3.8 trillion), in Japan ($1.6 trillion), in Germany ($908.0 billion), in France ($628.2 billion), and in the UK ($592.3 billion). The value of services per capita in Brazil was less than in the USA ($14.4 thousand), in Japan ($12.8 thousand), in Germany ($11.3 thousand), in France ($10.6 thousand), and in the UK ($10.2 thousand). The growth of services in Brazil was greater than in Japan (1.7%) and in France (1.6%); but less than in Germany (3.2%), in the United Kingdom (3.0%), and in the United States (2.3%).

The 2000s

The Brazilian services were $387.0 billion per year in the 2000s, ranked 10th in the world. The share in the world was 2.0%, and 4.7% in the Americas.

The share of services in the economy of Brazil was 46.8% in the 2000s, ranked 32nd in the world, and was on a par with Micronesia (46.8%), Italy (46.6%), the FSM (46.6%).

The services per capita in Brazil were $2 094.6 in the 2000s, ranked 78th in the world, and were on a par with Western Asia ($2.1 thousand), the Caribbean ($2.0 thousand), Eastern Asia ($2.0 thousand). The value added of services per capita in Brazil was less than services per capita in the world ($3 011.2) by 30.4%, and was less than services per capita in the Americas ($9 407.5) in 4.5 times.

The growth of services in Brazil was 2.9% in the 2000s, ranked 141st in the world, and was on a par with the World (2.9%), Kyrgyzstan (2.9%), Israel (2.9%). The growth of services in Brazil (2.9%) was greater than growth of services in the world (2.9%), was greater than growth of services in the Americas (2.2%).

Comparison with neighbors. The value added of services in Brazil was greater than in Argentina ($78.8 billion), in Colombia ($50.2 billion), in Venezuela ($42.6 billion), in Peru ($22.4 billion), in Uruguay ($7.9 billion), in Paraguay ($3.3 billion), and in Bolivia ($2.9

Chapter IX. Services

billion). The Brazilian services per capita were greater than in Argentina ($2.0 thousand), in Venezuela ($1 629.3), in Colombia ($1 187.0), in Peru ($809.1), in Paraguay ($568.8), and in Bolivia ($313.8); but less than in Uruguay ($2.4 thousand). The growth of services in Brazil was greater than in Peru (2.8%), in Bolivia (2.3%), in Argentina (2.2%), in Paraguay (2.0%), and in Uruguay (0.85%); but less than in Venezuela (5.0%) and in Colombia (3.6%).

Comparison with leaders. The value of services in Brazil was less than in the USA ($6.7 trillion), in Japan ($2.0 trillion), in Germany ($1.2 trillion), in the UK ($1.1 trillion), and in France ($997.0 billion). The value added of services per capita in Brazil was less than in the United States ($22.9 thousand), in the United Kingdom ($18.0 thousand), in France ($15.9 thousand), in Japan ($15.3 thousand), and in Germany ($15.0 thousand). The growth of services in Brazil was greater than in the United Kingdom (2.7%), in the United States (2.0%), in France (1.5%), in Japan (1.2%), and in Germany (0.57%).

The 2010s

The Brazil's services were $879.0 billion per year in the 2010s, ranked 8th in the world. The share in the world was 2.7%, and 6.8% in the Americas.

The share of services in the economy of Brazil was 47.5% in the 2010s, ranked 40th in the world, and was on a par with Switzerland (47.7%), Sweden (47.7%), Spain (47.3%).

The services per capita in Brazil were $4 318.9 in the 2010s, ranked 75th in the world, and were on a par with Trinidad and Tobago ($4.3 thousand), Argentina ($4.4 thousand). The Brazil's services per capita were less than services per capita in the world ($4 467.8) by 3.3%, and were less than services per capita in the Americas ($13 184.6) in 3.1 times.

The growth of services in Brazil was 1.8% in the 2010s, ranked 139th in the world, and was on a par with Liechtenstein (1.8%), the Americas (1.8%), Lithuania (1.8%). The growth of services in Brazil (1.8%) was less than growth of services in the world (2.7%), was greater than growth of services in the Americas (1.8%).

Comparison with neighbors. The services of Brazil were 4.7 times higher than in Argentina ($187.4 billion), 7.5 times higher than in Colombia ($117.5 billion), 11.8 times higher than in Venezuela ($74.5 billion), 15.4 times higher than in Peru ($57.0 billion), 40.8 times higher than in Uruguay ($21.5 billion), 89.4 times higher than in Paraguay ($9.8 billion), and 99.0 times higher than in Bolivia ($8.9 billion). The Brazil's services per capita were 69.9% higher than in Venezuela ($2.5 thousand), 74.7% higher than in Colombia ($2.5 thousand), 2.3 times higher than in Peru ($1 869.0), 2.9 times higher than in Paraguay ($1 479.6), and 5.2 times higher than in Bolivia ($823.3); but 31.6% lower than in Uruguay ($6.3 thousand) and 1.2% lower than in Argentina ($4.4 thousand). The growth of services in Brazil was greater than in Argentina (1.8%) and in Venezuela (-8.0%); but less than in Bolivia (5.7%), in Peru (5.0%), in Paraguay (4.4%), in Colombia (4.3%), and in Uruguay (1.9%).

Comparison with leaders. The value added of services in Brazil was 11.3 times lower than in the USA ($10.0 trillion), 4.0 times lower than in China ($3.5 trillion), 2.6 times lower than in Japan ($2.3 trillion), 45.3% lower than in Germany ($1.6 trillion), and 35.1% lower than in the UK ($1.4 trillion). The value added of services per capita in Brazil was 70.8% higher than in China ($2.5 thousand); but 7.2 times lower than in the United States ($31.2 thousand), 4.8 times lower than in the UK ($20.7 thousand), 4.5 times lower than in Germany ($19.6 thousand), and 4.1 times lower than in Japan ($17.8 thousand). The growth of services in Brazil was greater than in the USA (1.8%), in the UK (1.7%), in Germany (1.2%), and in Japan (0.99%); but less than in China (8.4%).

Part III. External relations

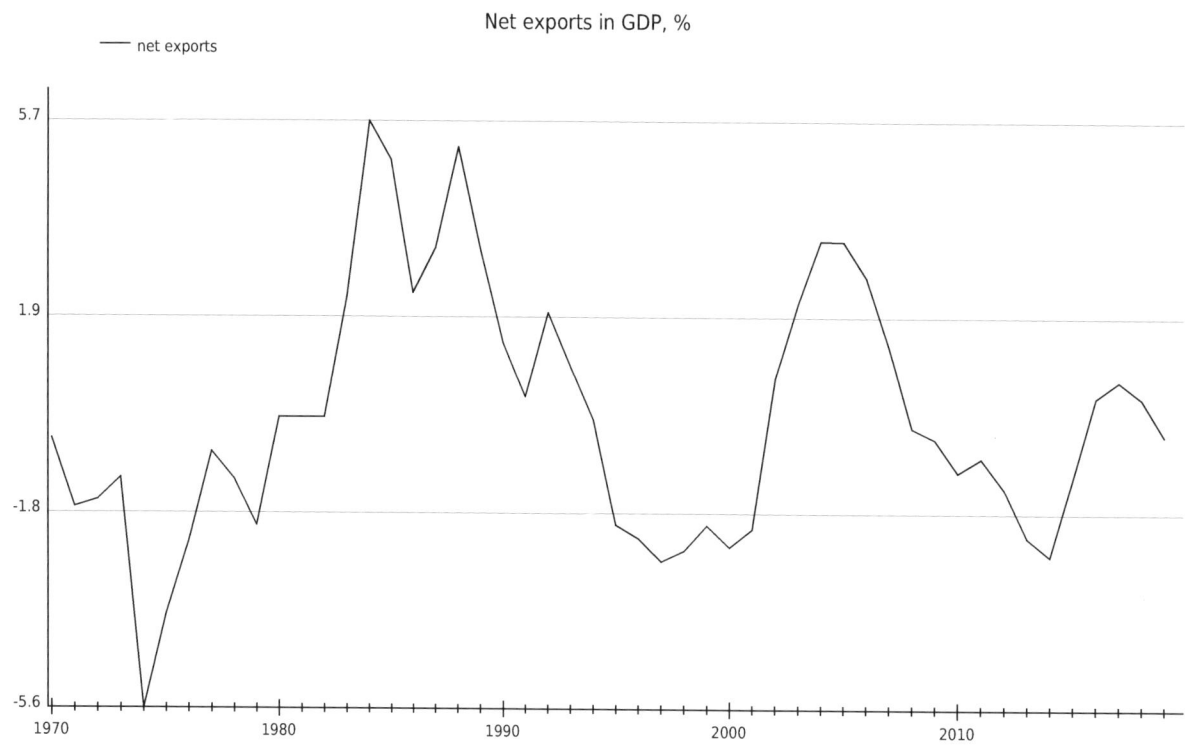

Chapter X. Exports

Exports of goods and services

The exports of Brazil grew up from $7.4 billion per year in the 1970s to $264.4 billion per year in the 2010s, that is by $257.0 billion or 35.9 times. The change occurred at $162.3 billion due to a 2.6-fold increase in prices, as also at $88.0 billion due to a 7.2-fold increase in per capita rate, as well as at $6.8 billion due to the increase in population. The average annual growth in exports is 6.6%. The minimum value of exports was in 1970 at $2.5 billion. The maximum value of exports was in 2011 at $300.0 billion.

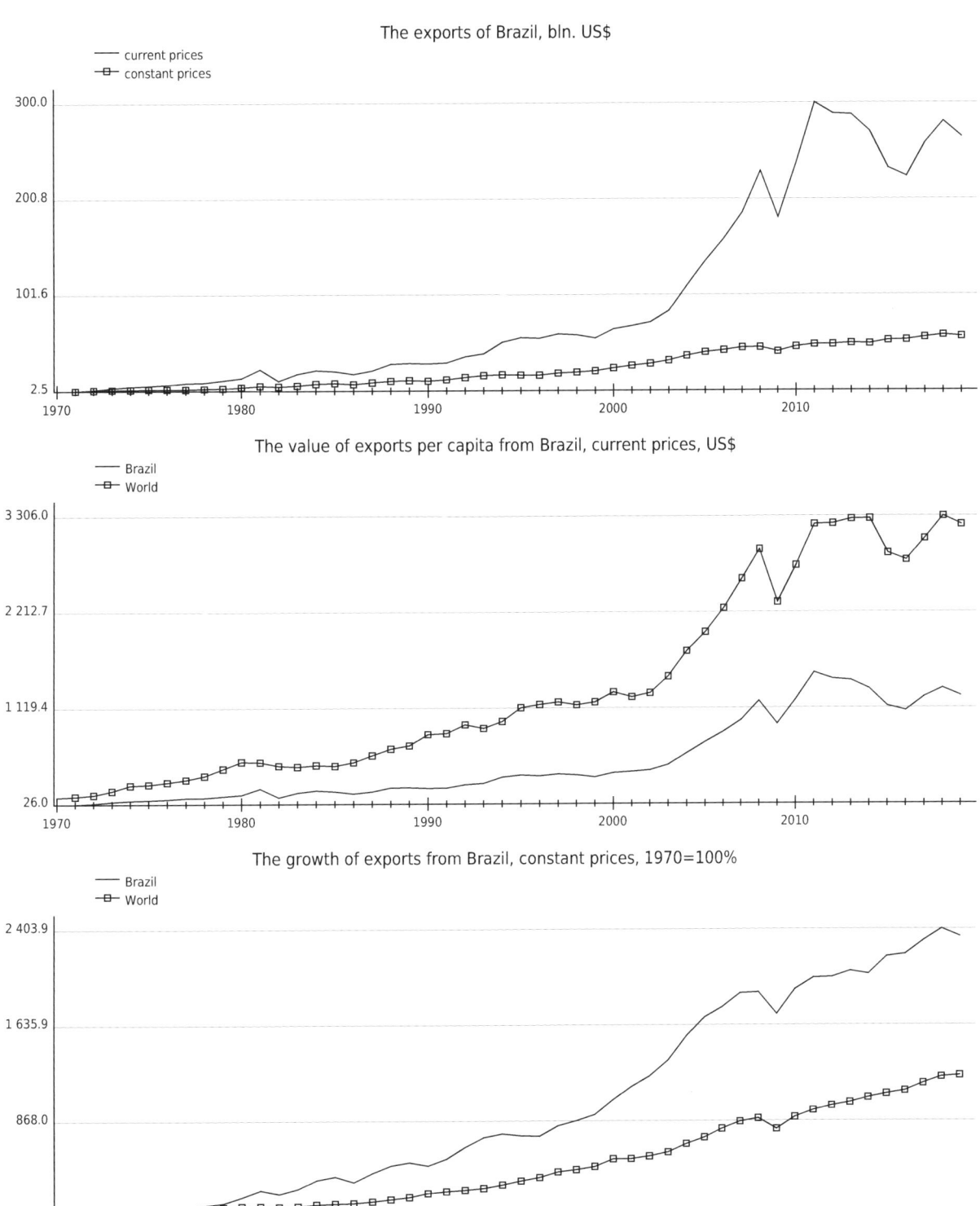

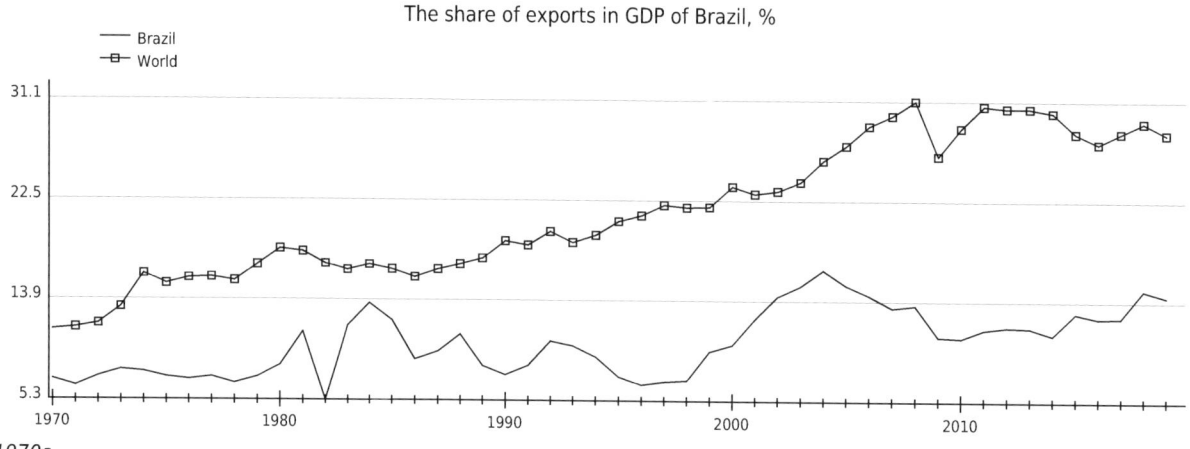

The share of exports in GDP of Brazil, %

The 1970s

The value of exports from Brazil was $7.4 billion per year in the 1970s, ranked 30th in the world, and was on a par with Nigeria ($7.5 billion), Indonesia ($7.5 billion), Middle Africa ($7.2 billion). The share in the world was 0.75%, and 3.3% from the Americas.

The share of exports in GDP of Brazil was 7.2% in the 1970s, ranked 171st in the world.

The exports per capita from Brazil were $69.4 in the 1970s, ranked 140th in the world, and were on a par with the Central African Republic ($70.3). The exports per capita from Brazil were less than exports per capita in the world ($242.1) in 3.5 times, and were less than exports per capita from the Americas ($397.2) in 5.7 times.

The growth of exports from Brazil was 8.6% in the 1970s, ranked 46th in the world, and was on a par with Mexico (8.6%), Japan (8.6%). The growth of exports from Brazil (8.6%) was greater than growth of exports in the world (6.5%), was greater than growth of exports from the Americas (6.4%).

Comparison with neighbors. The exports of Brazil were greater than from Argentina ($3.5 billion), from Colombia ($2.2 billion), from Peru ($2.0 billion), from Uruguay ($581.0 million), from Bolivia ($546.1 million), and from Paraguay ($347.3 million); but less than from Venezuela ($8.7 billion). The value of exports per capita from Brazil was less than from Venezuela ($667.2), from Uruguay ($204.6), from Argentina ($137.3), from Peru ($133.2), from Paraguay ($125.4), from Bolivia ($110.2), and from Colombia ($90.7). The growth of exports from Brazil was greater than from Uruguay (7.6%), from Colombia (6.4%), from Argentina (5.9%), from Peru (4.1%), and from Bolivia (3.7%); but less than from Paraguay (13.6%) and from Venezuela (9.0%).

Comparison with leaders. The Brazil's exports were less than from the USA ($128.0 billion), from Germany ($82.9 billion), from France ($64.3 billion), from Japan ($64.1 billion), and from the UK ($61.3 billion). The Brazilian exports per capita were less than from France ($1 199.1), from the United Kingdom ($1 094.1), from Germany ($1 052.2), from the USA ($586.5), and from Japan ($575.8). The growth of exports from Brazil was greater than from France (7.8%), from the USA (6.8%), from Germany (5.1%), and from the UK (5.0%); but less than from Japan (8.6%).

The 1980s

The value of exports from Brazil was $22.4 billion per year in the 1980s, ranked 26th in the world, and was on a par with Western Africa ($22.1 billion), South Africa ($23.0 billion). The share in the world was 0.88%, and 3.8% from the Americas.

The share of exports in GDP of Brazil was 9.7% in the 1980s, ranked 161st in the world, and was on a par with Northern America (9.7%), Guinea-Bissau (9.7%), China (9.7%).

The exports per capita from Brazil were $167.8 in the 1980s, ranked 131st in the world, and were on a par with the Comoros ($164.3), Nigeria ($163.8). The Brazilian exports per capita were less than exports per capita in the world ($529.9) in 3.2 times, and were less than exports per capita from the Americas ($890.9) in 5.3 times.

The growth of exports from Brazil was 9.8% in the 1980s, ranked 23rd in the world. The growth of exports from Brazil (9.8%) was greater than growth of exports in the world (3.8%), was greater than growth of exports from the Americas (5.1%).

Comparison with neighbors. The value of exports from Brazil was greater than from Venezuela ($16.4 billion), from Argentina ($8.1 billion), from Colombia ($5.1 billion), from Peru ($4.2 billion), from Paraguay ($1.5 billion), from Uruguay ($1.4 billion), and from

Chapter X. Exports

Bolivia ($1.1 billion). The Brazil's exports per capita were less than from Venezuela ($957.3), from Uruguay ($479.2), from Paraguay ($403.8), from Argentina ($269.9), from Peru ($212.9), from Bolivia ($185.1), and from Colombia ($173.1). The growth of exports from Brazil was greater than from Colombia (4.9%), from Paraguay (4.2%), from Uruguay (3.8%), from Argentina (2.9%), from Bolivia (1.1%), from Venezuela (-0.63%), and from Peru (-1.2%).

Comparison with leaders. The value of exports from Brazil was less than from the USA ($338.6 billion), from Japan ($210.6 billion), from Germany ($208.1 billion), from France ($155.9 billion), and from the United Kingdom ($155.0 billion). The Brazil's exports per capita were less than from France ($2.8 thousand), from the UK ($2.7 thousand), from Germany ($2.7 thousand), from Japan ($1 736.5), and from the United States ($1 413.8). The growth of exports from Brazil was greater than from Japan (6.7%), from the USA (5.7%), from Germany (4.7%), from France (4.0%), and from the United Kingdom (3.0%).

The 1990s

The value of exports from Brazil was $48.3 billion per year in the 1990s, ranked 28th in the world, and was on a par with Ireland ($49.2 billion). The share in the world was 0.82%, and 3.8% from the Americas.

The share of exports in GDP of Brazil was 7.9% in the 1990s, ranked 202nd in the world, and was on a par with Ethiopia (7.9%).

The exports per capita from Brazil were $300.8 in the 1990s, ranked 135th in the world, and were on a par with Colombia ($300.7), Guatemala ($298.4). The value of exports per capita from Brazil was less than exports per capita in the world ($1 029.5) in 3.4 times, and was less than exports per capita from the Americas ($1 662.5) in 5.5 times.

The growth of exports from Brazil was 5.5% in the 1990s, ranked 94th in the world, and was on a par with Swaziland (5.5%), Morocco (5.5%), Dominica (5.5%). The growth of exports from Brazil (5.5%) was less than growth of exports in the world (6.9%), was less than growth of exports from the Americas (7.3%).

Comparison with neighbors. The Brazilian exports were greater than from Argentina ($22.4 billion), from Venezuela ($19.9 billion), from Colombia ($10.8 billion), from Peru ($6.1 billion), from Paraguay ($3.4 billion), from Uruguay ($3.2 billion), and from Bolivia ($1.4 billion). The exports per capita from Brazil were greater than from Colombia ($300.7), from Peru ($253.8), and from Bolivia ($181.6); but less than from Uruguay ($991.2), from Venezuela ($918.3), from Paraguay ($726.8), and from Argentina ($648.4). The growth of exports from Brazil was greater than from Venezuela (5.0%), from Bolivia (4.2%), and from Paraguay (3.2%); but less than from Argentina (8.0%), from Colombia (6.6%), from Uruguay (6.2%), and from Peru (5.9%).

Comparison with leaders. The Brazil's exports were less than from the United States ($773.6 billion), from Germany ($509.0 billion), from Japan ($418.7 billion), from France ($329.8 billion), and from the United Kingdom ($324.3 billion). The value of exports per capita from Brazil was less than from Germany ($6.3 thousand), from the United Kingdom ($5.6 thousand), from France ($5.6 thousand), from Japan ($3.3 thousand), and from the United States ($2.9 thousand). The growth of exports from Brazil was greater than from Japan (4.2%); but less than from the USA (7.2%), from France (6.5%), from Germany (6.0%), and from the United Kingdom (5.7%).

The 2000s

The exports of Brazil were $129.5 billion per year in the 2000s, ranked 26th in the world, and were on a par with Thailand ($130.0 billion). The share in the world was 1.0%, and 5.3% from the Americas.

The structure of exports: primary products (27.7%), resource-based manufactures (28.1%), low technology manufactures (9.2%), medium technology manufactures (24.4%), and high technology manufactures (8.0%).

Brazil exported goods to the United States (18.1%), Argentina (8.5%), China (7.3%), the Netherlands (5.3%), Germany (4.4%) and other countries (56.5%).

The share of exports in GDP of Brazil was 13.3% in the 2000s, ranked 198th in the world, and was on a par with São Tomé and Príncipe (13.3%), Japan (13.4%).

The Brazilian exports per capita were $701.0 in the 2000s, ranked 130th in the world, and were on a par with Cuba ($688.4), Honduras ($719.0). The value of exports per capita from Brazil was less than exports per capita in the world ($1 933.7) in 2.8 times, and was less than exports per capita from the Americas ($2 781.7) in 4.0 times.

The growth of exports from Brazil was 6.5% in the 2000s, ranked 74th in the world. The growth of exports from Brazil (6.5%) was greater than growth of exports in the world (4.8%), was greater than growth of exports from the Americas (2.9%).

Comparison with neighbors. The value of exports from Brazil was greater than from Venezuela ($51.3 billion), from Argentina ($47.6 billion), from Colombia ($25.0 billion), from Peru ($20.1 billion), from Uruguay ($5.4 billion), from Paraguay ($5.3 billion), and from Bolivia ($3.7 billion). The Brazilian exports per capita were greater than from Colombia ($591.6) and from Bolivia ($404.6); but less than from Venezuela ($1 961.5), from Uruguay ($1 610.4), from Argentina ($1 229.8), from Paraguay ($919.7), and from Peru ($724.8). The growth of exports from Brazil was greater than from Colombia (4.1%), from Argentina (3.9%), and from Venezuela (-2.3%); but less than from Paraguay (7.8%), from Uruguay (6.9%), from Bolivia (6.9%), and from Peru (6.9%).

Comparison with leaders. The exports of Brazil were less than from the United States ($1.3 trillion), from Germany ($1.0 trillion), from China ($780.2 billion), from Japan ($626.3 billion), and from the United Kingdom ($591.1 billion). The value of exports per capita from Brazil was greater than from China ($588.1); but less than from Germany ($12.8 thousand), from the UK ($9.8 thousand), from Japan ($4.9 thousand), and from the USA ($4.5 thousand). The growth of exports from Brazil was greater than from Germany (5.0%), from Japan (3.5%), from the USA (3.3%), and from the UK (2.8%); but less than from China (12.7%).

The 2010s

The exports of Brazil were $264.4 billion per year in the 2010s, ranked 24th in the world. The share in the world was 1.2%, and 6.5% from the Americas.

The structure of exports: primary products (35.5%), resource-based manufactures (31.5%), low technology manufactures (5.4%), medium technology manufactures (20.1%), and high technology manufactures (4.5%).

Brazil exported goods to China (19.6%), the USA (11.6%), Argentina (7.7%), the Netherlands (5.7%), Japan (3.0%) and other countries (52.4%).

The share of exports in GDP of Brazil was 12.2% in the 2010s, ranked 201st in the world.

The exports per capita from Brazil were $1 299.0 in the 2010s, ranked 137th in the world, and were on a par with Samoa ($1 309.6), Albania ($1 321.7). The exports per capita from Brazil were less than exports per capita in the world ($3 098.9) in 2.4 times, and were less than exports per capita from the Americas ($4 197.2) in 3.2 times.

The growth of exports from Brazil was 3.1% in the 2010s, ranked 129th in the world, and was on a par with Grenada (3.1%), the UK (3.1%), Guinea-Bissau (3.1%). The growth of exports from Brazil (3.1%) was less than growth of exports in the world (4.4%), was less than growth of exports from the Americas (3.6%).

Comparison with neighbors. The value of exports from Brazil was 3.3 times higher than from Argentina ($80.7 billion), 4.8 times higher than from Colombia ($55.3 billion), 5.1 times higher than from Venezuela ($52.1 billion), 5.4 times higher than from Peru ($48.9 billion), 20.1 times higher than from Paraguay ($13.1 billion), 21.3 times higher than from Uruguay ($12.4 billion), and 24.5 times higher than from Bolivia ($10.8 billion). The value of exports per capita from Brazil was 11.6% higher than from Colombia ($1 164.0) and 30.0% higher than from Bolivia ($999.1); but 2.8 times lower than from Uruguay ($3.6 thousand), 34.3% lower than from Paraguay ($1 977.2), 31.1% lower than from Argentina ($1 884.5), 26.9% lower than from Venezuela ($1 777.6), and 18.9% lower than from Peru ($1 602.5). The growth of exports from Brazil was greater than from Colombia (3.1%), from Bolivia (2.7%), from Uruguay (2.2%), from Argentina (1.5%), and from Venezuela (-8.8%); but less than from Paraguay (4.1%) and from Peru (3.6%).

Comparison with leaders. The exports of Brazil were 8.7 times lower than from China ($2.3 trillion), 8.6 times lower than from the USA ($2.3 trillion), 6.4 times lower than from Germany ($1.7 trillion), 3.3 times lower than from Japan ($859.4 billion), and 3.1 times lower than from the UK ($815.1 billion). The Brazilian exports per capita were 15.8 times lower than from Germany ($20.6 thousand), 9.6 times lower than from the UK ($12.4 thousand), 5.5 times lower than from the United States ($7.1 thousand), 5.2 times lower than from Japan ($6.7 thousand), and 20.6% lower than from China ($1 635.3). The growth of exports from Brazil was greater than from the United Kingdom (3.1%); but less than from China (6.8%), from Germany (4.7%), from Japan (4.6%), and from the United States (3.7%).

Chapter XI. Imports

Imports of goods and services

The value of imports in Brazil increased from $9.5 billion per year in the 1970s to $284.0 billion per year in the 2010s, that is by $274.5 billion or 29.8 times. The change occurred at $212.5 billion due to a 4.0-fold increase in prices, as also at $53.3 billion due to a 3.9-fold increase in per capita rate, as well as at $8.7 billion due to the growth in population. The average annual growth in imports is 5.4%. The minimum value of imports was in 1970 at $2.6 billion. The maximum value of imports was in 2013 at $344.5 billion.

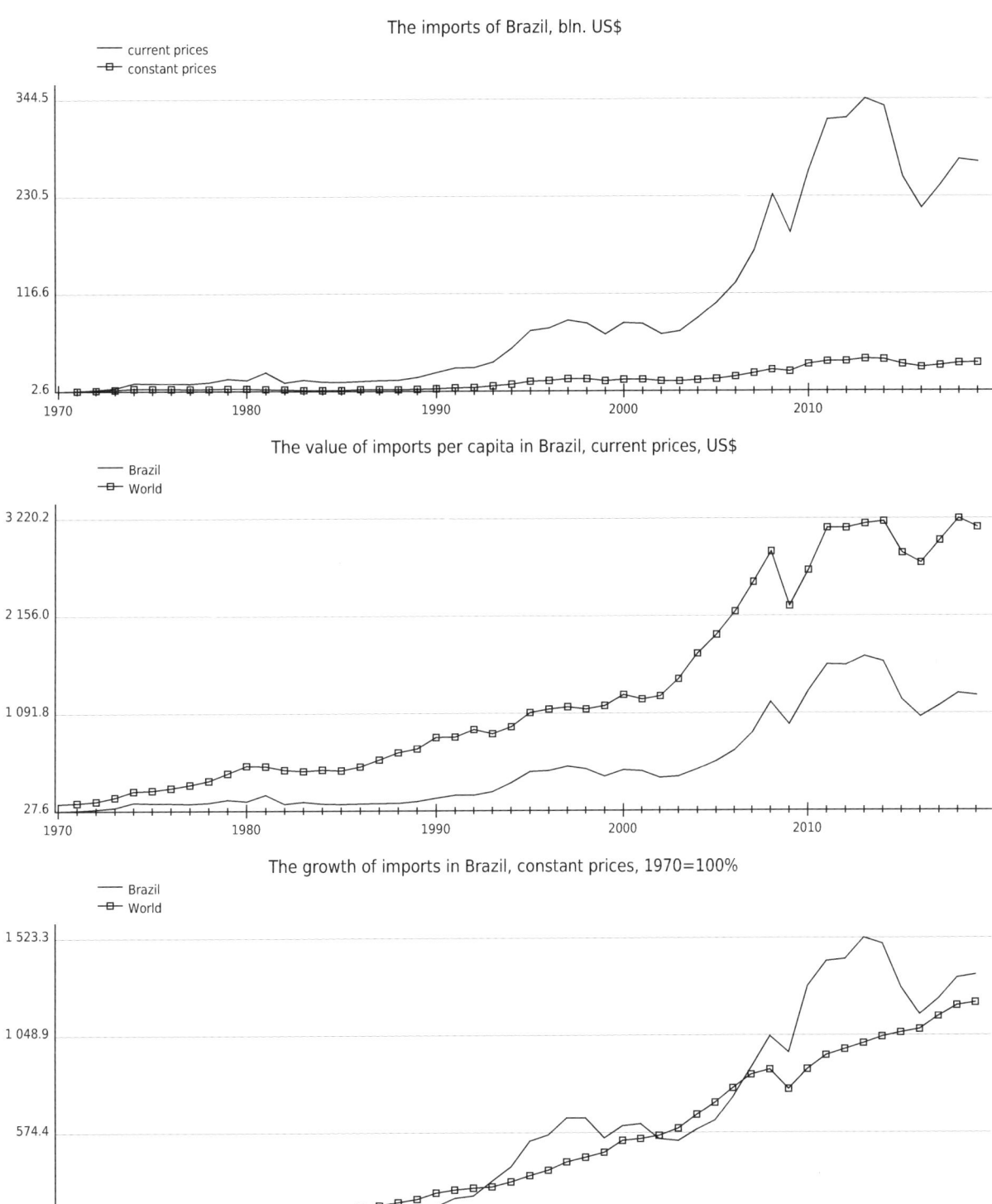

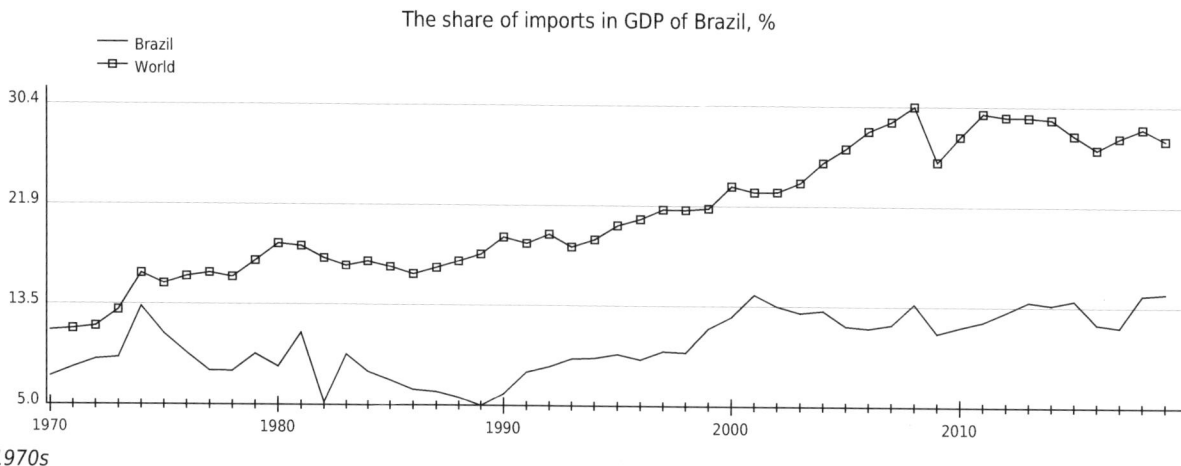

The 1970s

The imports of Brazil were $9.5 billion per year in the 1970s, ranked 21st in the world. The share in the world was 0.97%, and 4.0% in the Americas.

The share of imports in GDP of Brazil was 9.3% in the 1970s, ranked 174th in the world.

The Brazilian imports per capita were $89.8 in the 1970s, ranked 145th in the world, and were on a par with the Philippines ($89.3), South-Eastern Asia ($91.2). The imports per capita in Brazil were less than imports per capita in the world ($244.3) in 2.7 times, and were less than imports per capita in the Americas ($421.7) in 4.7 times.

The growth of imports in Brazil was 9.1% in the 1970s, ranked 43rd in the world, and was on a par with Mauritania (9.1%), Aruba (9.1%). The growth of imports in Brazil (9.1%) was greater than growth of imports in the world (6.3%), was greater than growth of imports in the Americas (5.4%).

Comparison with neighbors. The Brazil's imports were greater than in Venezuela ($8.0 billion), in Colombia ($2.9 billion), in Argentina ($2.9 billion), in Peru ($2.4 billion), in Uruguay ($760.2 million), in Bolivia ($594.7 million), and in Paraguay ($338.3 million). The Brazilian imports per capita were less than in Venezuela ($611.9), in Uruguay ($267.7), in Peru ($158.3), in Paraguay ($122.2), in Colombia ($120.2), in Bolivia ($120.0), and in Argentina ($111.4). The growth of imports in Brazil was greater than in Argentina (6.7%), in Colombia (5.3%), in Uruguay (4.9%), in Bolivia (3.9%), in Venezuela (3.8%), and in Peru (-0.55%); but less than in Paraguay (13.1%).

Comparison with leaders. The imports of Brazil were less than in the United States ($133.2 billion), in Germany ($92.5 billion), in France ($63.3 billion), in the UK ($62.4 billion), and in Japan ($61.0 billion). The value of imports per capita in Brazil was less than in France ($1 181.1), in Germany ($1 175.1), in the United Kingdom ($1 113.2), in the USA ($610.4), and in Japan ($547.6). The growth of imports in Brazil was greater than in France (7.2%), in Japan (7.0%), in Germany (5.6%), in the USA (5.1%), and in the United Kingdom (4.5%).

The 1980s

The Brazil's imports were $16.1 billion per year in the 1980s, ranked 31st in the world. The share in the world was 0.62%, and 2.5% in the Americas.

The share of imports in GDP of Brazil was 7.0% in the 1980s, ranked 181st in the world.

The Brazilian imports per capita were $120.5 in the 1980s, ranked 152nd in the world, and were on a par with El Salvador ($119.7), Guinea ($119.3), Benin ($122.9). The imports per capita in Brazil were less than imports per capita in the world ($539.1) in 4.5 times, and were less than imports per capita in the Americas ($984.9) in 8.2 times.

The growth of imports in Brazil was -1.1% in the 1980s, ranked 154th in the world. The growth of imports in Brazil (-1.1%) was less than growth of imports in the world (3.8%), was less than growth of imports in the Americas (3.8%).

Comparison with neighbors. The imports of Brazil were greater than in Venezuela ($13.4 billion), in Colombia ($7.3 billion), in Argentina ($5.8 billion), in Peru ($4.5 billion), in Uruguay ($1.6 billion), in Paraguay ($1.5 billion), and in Bolivia ($874.9 million). The Brazilian imports per capita were less than in Venezuela ($780.0), in Uruguay ($528.5), in Paraguay ($408.8), in Colombia ($245.1),

Chapter XI. Imports

in Peru ($231.1), in Argentina ($194.4), and in Bolivia ($142.7). The growth of imports in Brazil was greater than in Venezuela (-2.3%) and in Argentina (-4.1%); but less than in Paraguay (3.5%), in Colombia (2.2%), in Uruguay (-0.34%), in Peru (-0.36%), and in Bolivia (-0.37%).

Comparison with leaders. The imports of Brazil were less than in the United States ($417.2 billion), in Germany ($225.6 billion), in Japan ($175.9 billion), in France ($162.0 billion), and in the United Kingdom ($157.7 billion). The Brazilian imports per capita were less than in Germany ($2.9 thousand), in France ($2.9 thousand), in the United Kingdom ($2.8 thousand), in the USA ($1 742.4), and in Japan ($1 450.4). The growth of imports in Brazil was less than in the United States (5.8%), in the UK (5.1%), in Japan (4.6%), in France (4.3%), and in Germany (3.3%).

The 1990s

The Brazil's imports were $55.9 billion per year in the 1990s, ranked 23rd in the world, and were on a par with Northern Africa ($56.7 billion). The share in the world was 0.97%, and 4.0% in the Americas.

The share of imports in GDP of Brazil was 9.2% in the 1990s, ranked 205th in the world.

The value of imports per capita in Brazil was $348.1 in the 1990s, ranked 147th in the world, and was on a par with Iran ($348.2), Northern Africa ($355.1). The imports per capita in Brazil were less than imports per capita in the world ($1 015.5) in 2.9 times, and were less than imports per capita in the Americas ($1 812.7) in 5.2 times.

The growth of imports in Brazil was 10.8% in the 1990s, ranked 24th in the world, and was on a par with Turkey (10.9%), Hungary (10.9%). The growth of imports in Brazil (10.8%) was greater than growth of imports in the world (6.6%), was greater than growth of imports in the Americas (8.2%).

Comparison with neighbors. The Brazil's imports were greater than in Argentina ($25.0 billion), in Colombia ($16.8 billion), in Venezuela ($15.9 billion), in Peru ($7.8 billion), in Paraguay ($4.0 billion), in Uruguay ($3.6 billion), and in Bolivia ($1.9 billion). The Brazilian imports per capita were greater than in Peru ($325.5) and in Bolivia ($247.7); but less than in Uruguay ($1 133.6), in Paraguay ($849.9), in Venezuela ($732.3), in Argentina ($721.5), and in Colombia ($466.9). The growth of imports in Brazil was greater than in Uruguay (10.0%), in Paraguay (8.9%), in Peru (8.8%), in Colombia (8.0%), in Venezuela (7.3%), and in Bolivia (6.2%); but less than in Argentina (17.8%).

Comparison with leaders. The value of imports in Brazil was less than in the USA ($874.1 billion), in Germany ($501.6 billion), in Japan ($355.9 billion), in the United Kingdom ($330.2 billion), and in France ($308.5 billion). The imports per capita in Brazil were less than in Germany ($6.2 thousand), in the United Kingdom ($5.7 thousand), in France ($5.2 thousand), in the USA ($3.3 thousand), and in Japan ($2.8 thousand). The growth of imports in Brazil was greater than in the USA (8.3%), in Germany (6.4%), in France (5.1%), in the United Kingdom (5.1%), and in Japan (3.3%).

The 2000s

The value of imports in Brazil was $121.5 billion per year in the 2000s, ranked 24th in the world, and was on a par with Northern Africa ($121.9 billion), Thailand ($119.6 billion). The share in the world was 0.98%, and 4.1% in the Americas.

The structure of imports: primary products (18.6%), resource-based manufactures (17.2%), low technology manufactures (7.3%), medium technology manufactures (35.2%), and high technology manufactures (20.6%).

Brazil imported goods from the United States (21.1%), Argentina (8.8%), Germany (8.0%), China (7.5%), Japan (3.5%) and other countries (51.1%).

The share of imports in GDP of Brazil was 12.5% in the 2000s, ranked 207th in the world.

The imports per capita in Brazil were $657.5 in the 2000s, ranked 146th in the world, and were on a par with East Timor ($656.3), Papua New Guinea ($648.5). The imports per capita in Brazil were less than imports per capita in the world ($1 899.9) in 2.9 times, and were less than imports per capita in the Americas ($3 354.4) in 5.1 times.

The growth of imports in Brazil was 5.8% in the 2000s, ranked 91st in the world. The growth of imports in Brazil (5.8%) was greater than growth of imports in the world (5.1%), was greater than growth of imports in the Americas (3.5%).

Comparison with neighbors. The imports of Brazil were greater than in Argentina ($36.4 billion), in Venezuela ($35.9 billion), in Colombia ($30.4 billion), in Peru ($17.3 billion), in Uruguay ($5.5 billion), in Paraguay ($4.6 billion), and in Bolivia ($3.4 billion). The imports per capita in Brazil were greater than in Peru ($623.6) and in Bolivia ($375.2); but less than in Uruguay ($1 664.0), in Venezuela ($1 373.0), in Argentina ($939.7), in Paraguay ($792.5), and in Colombia ($718.7). The growth of imports in Brazil was greater than in Paraguay (4.6%), in Bolivia (4.0%), in Uruguay (3.8%), and in Argentina (1.7%); but less than in Venezuela (9.0%), in Colombia (7.8%), and in Peru (7.1%).

Comparison with leaders. The imports of Brazil were less than in the USA ($1.9 trillion), in Germany ($914.7 billion), in the United Kingdom ($641.8 billion), in China ($641.1 billion), and in Japan ($566.4 billion). The imports per capita in Brazil were greater than in China ($483.3); but less than in Germany ($11.2 thousand), in the UK ($10.6 thousand), in the United States ($6.4 thousand), and in Japan ($4.4 thousand). The growth of imports in Brazil was greater than in Germany (3.7%), in the United Kingdom (3.1%), in the United States (2.8%), and in Japan (1.8%); but less than in China (15.1%).

The 2010s

The imports of Brazil were $284.0 billion per year in the 2010s, ranked 20th in the world. The share in the world was 1.3%, and 6.0% in the Americas.

The structure of imports: primary products (15.2%), resource-based manufactures (18.5%), low technology manufactures (9.2%), medium technology manufactures (38.0%), and high technology manufactures (18.9%).

Brazil imported goods from the United States (19.4%), China (15.2%), Argentina (6.6%), Germany (6.5%), Republic of Korea (3.9%) and other countries (48.4%).

The share of imports in GDP of Brazil was 13.1% in the 2010s, ranked 209th in the world.

The value of imports per capita in Brazil was $1 395.6 in the 2010s, ranked 145th in the world, and was on a par with Honduras ($1 428.1), Colombia ($1 431.2). The Brazil's imports per capita were less than imports per capita in the world ($3 015.6) in 2.2 times, and were less than imports per capita in the Americas ($4 884.3) in 3.5 times.

The growth of imports in Brazil was 3.4% in the 2010s, ranked 130th in the world. The growth of imports in Brazil (3.4%) was less than growth of imports in the world (4.4%), was greater than growth of imports in the Americas (3.3%).

Comparison with neighbors. The value of imports in Brazil was 2.9 times higher than in Venezuela ($96.3 billion), 3.5 times higher than in Argentina ($80.5 billion), 4.2 times higher than in Colombia ($68.0 billion), 6.1 times higher than in Peru ($46.8 billion), 23.0 times higher than in Uruguay ($12.4 billion), 23.1 times higher than in Paraguay ($12.3 billion), and 25.4 times higher than in Bolivia ($11.2 billion). The Brazilian imports per capita were 34.6% higher than in Bolivia ($1 036.6); but 2.6 times lower than in Uruguay ($3.6 thousand), 2.4 times lower than in Venezuela ($3.3 thousand), 25.7% lower than in Argentina ($1 878.1), 24.5% lower than in Paraguay ($1 849.2), 9.0% lower than in Peru ($1 533.8), and 2.5% lower than in Colombia ($1 431.2). The growth of imports in Brazil was greater than in Uruguay (2.6%) and in Venezuela (-16.8%); but less than in Colombia (6.6%), in Peru (6.3%), in Bolivia (5.3%), in Paraguay (5.1%), and in Argentina (3.6%).

Comparison with leaders. The Brazilian imports were 9.9 times lower than in the USA ($2.8 trillion), 7.3 times lower than in China ($2.1 trillion), 5.1 times lower than in Germany ($1.5 trillion), 3.1 times lower than in Japan ($877.9 billion), and 3.0 times lower than in the UK ($854.8 billion). The value of imports per capita in Brazil was 12.7 times lower than in Germany ($17.8 thousand), 9.3 times lower than in the United Kingdom ($13.0 thousand), 6.3 times lower than in the United States ($8.8 thousand), 4.9 times lower than in Japan ($6.9 thousand), and 5.4% lower than in China ($1 475.4). The growth of imports in Brazil was less than in China (8.2%), in Germany (4.8%), in the USA (4.4%), in Japan (3.8%), and in the United Kingdom (3.6%).

Part IV. Consumption

Chapter XII. Government consumption expenditure

General government final consumption expenditure

The public expenditure of Brazil grew up from $10.3 billion per year in the 1970s to $419.5 billion per year in the 2010s, that is by $409.2 billion or 40.9 times. The change occurred at $393.0 billion due to a 15.9-fold increase in prices, as also at $6.8 billion due to a 1.3-fold increase in per capita rate, as well as at $9.4 billion due to the rise in population. The average annual growth in public expenditure is 2.9%. The minimum value of government expenditure was in 1970 at $4.0 billion. The maximum value of government consumption expenditure was in 2011 at $488.4 billion.

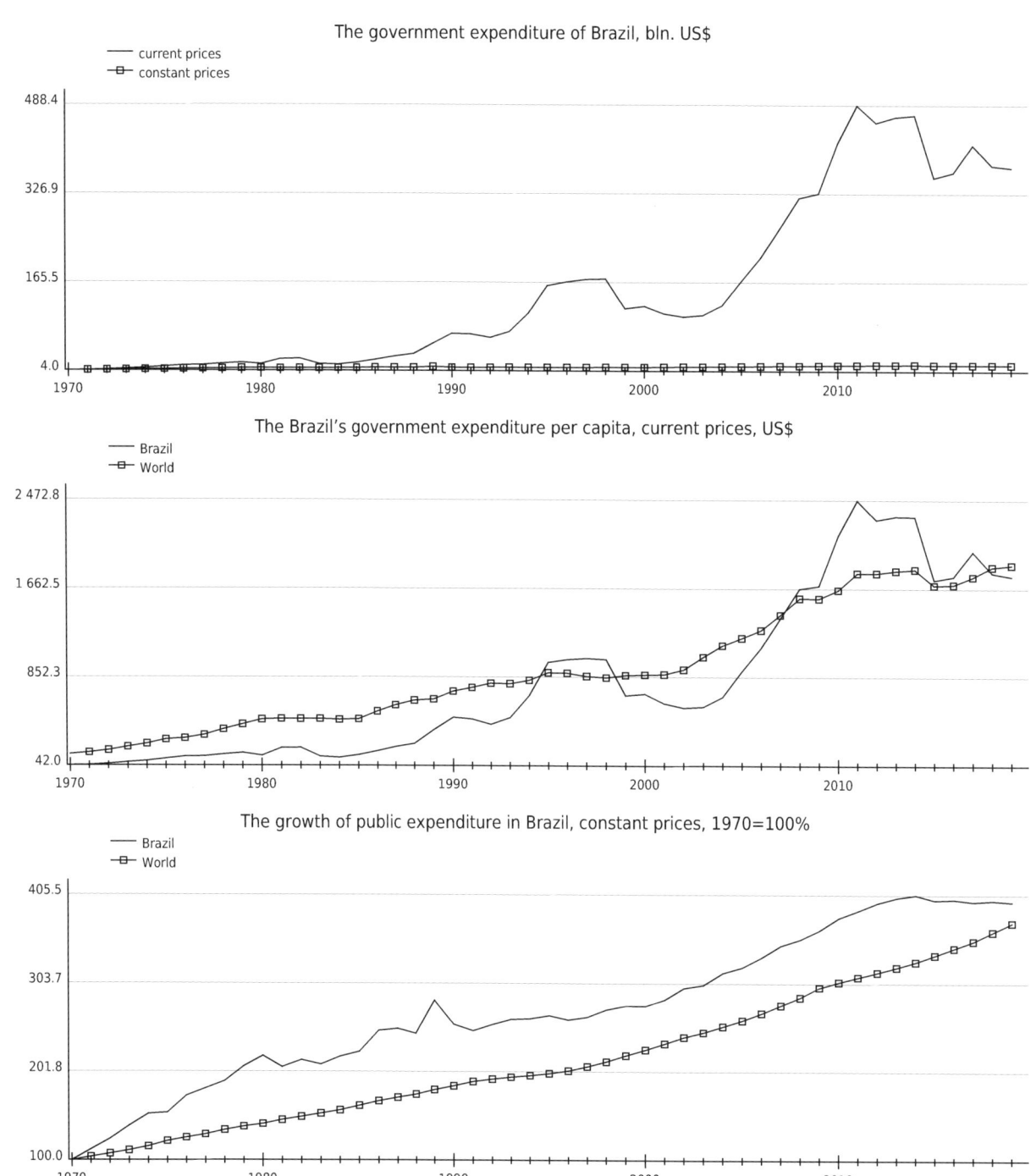

Chapter XII. Government consumption expenditure

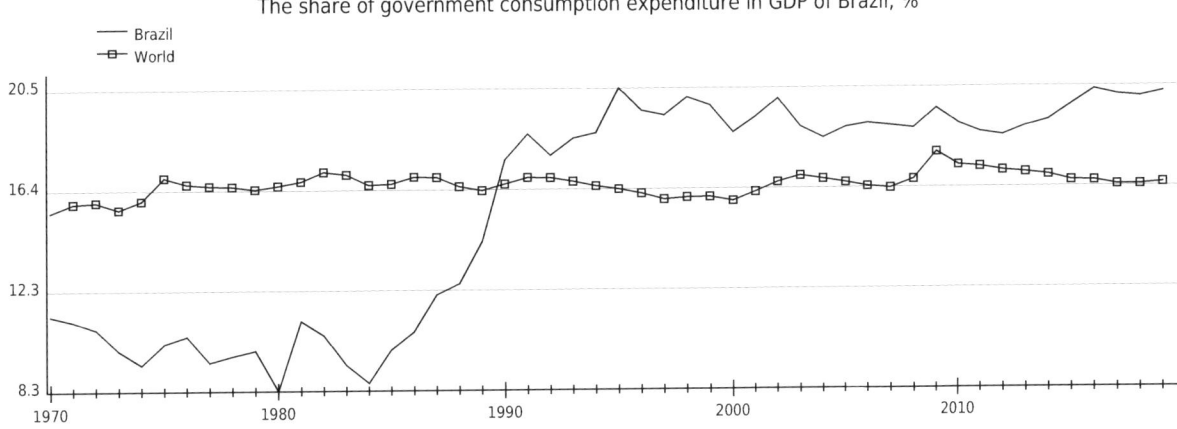

The 1970s

The Brazilian public expenditure was $10.3 billion per year in the 1970s, ranked 15th in the world, and was on a par with Iran ($10.2 billion). The share in the world was 0.96%, and 2.8% in the Americas.

The share of government expenditure in GDP of Brazil was 10.0% in the 1970s, ranked 151st in the world, and was on a par with Cyprus (9.9%), the Cayman Islands (10.1%).

The Brazilian government expenditure per capita was $96.7 in the 1970s, ranked 118th in the world, and was on a par with Mozambique ($96.9), Albania ($96.1), Middle Africa ($95.9). The Brazil's public expenditure per capita was less than public expenditure per capita in the world ($265.2) in 2.7 times, and was less than government expenditure per capita in the Americas ($655.5) in 6.8 times.

The growth of government consumption expenditure in Brazil was 8.5% in the 1970s, ranked 44th in the world, and was on a par with Central America (8.4%), Portugal (8.4%), Western Asia (8.5%). The growth of government expenditure in Brazil (8.5%) was greater than growth of public expenditure in the world (3.7%), was greater than growth of government expenditure in the Americas (2.1%).

Comparison with neighbors. The government consumption expenditure of Brazil was greater than in Venezuela ($6.5 billion), in Argentina ($4.7 billion), in Peru ($1.7 billion), in Colombia ($1.4 billion), in Uruguay ($513.4 million), in Bolivia ($247.0 million), and in Paraguay ($142.8 million). The Brazil's public expenditure per capita was greater than in Colombia ($58.3), in Paraguay ($51.6), and in Bolivia ($49.8); but less than in Venezuela ($495.6), in Argentina ($184.2), in Uruguay ($180.8), and in Peru ($109.9). The growth of government expenditure in Brazil was greater than in Colombia (6.5%), in Paraguay (4.3%), in Uruguay (3.9%), in Argentina (3.8%), in Peru (3.5%), and in Venezuela (3.3%); but less than in Bolivia (8.8%).

Comparison with leaders. The government expenditure of Brazil was less than in the United States ($285.9 billion), in the USSR ($117.3 billion), in Germany ($95.6 billion), in Japan ($78.0 billion), and in France ($64.5 billion). The Brazilian public expenditure per capita was less than in the United States ($1 310.2), in Germany ($1 213.7), in France ($1 202.3), in Japan ($700.2), and in the USSR ($465.0). The growth of public expenditure in Brazil was greater than in the USSR (7.2%), in Japan (5.3%), in France (5.0%), in Germany (4.4%), and in the United States (0.94%).

The 1980s

The public expenditure of Brazil was $25.9 billion per year in the 1980s, ranked 17th in the world, and was on a par with India ($26.2 billion), Northern Africa ($25.5 billion), Belgium ($26.4 billion). The share in the world was 1.0%, and 3.0% in the Americas.

The share of government expenditure in GDP of Brazil was 11.2% in the 1980s, ranked 144th in the world, and was on a par with Somalia (11.2%), Bermuda (11.1%).

The government consumption expenditure per capita in Brazil was $193.5 in the 1980s, ranked 115th in the world, and was on a par with Gambia ($197.6). The public expenditure per capita in Brazil was less than government expenditure per capita in the world ($523.5) in 2.7 times, and was less than government consumption expenditure per capita in the Americas ($1 287.2) in 6.7 times.

The growth of government consumption expenditure in Brazil was 3.2% in the 1980s, ranked 96th in the world, and was on a par with Central America (3.1%), Switzerland (3.2%). The growth of government consumption expenditure in Brazil (3.2%) was greater than growth of government expenditure in the world (2.7%), was greater than growth of government expenditure in the Americas (2.5%).

Comparison with neighbors. The government consumption expenditure of Brazil was greater than in Venezuela ($13.4 billion), in Argentina ($11.0 billion), in Colombia ($4.2 billion), in Peru ($3.7 billion), in Uruguay ($1.0 billion), in Paraguay ($499.8 million), and in Bolivia ($427.2 million). The government consumption expenditure per capita in Brazil was greater than in Peru ($188.2), in Colombia ($140.9), in Paraguay ($137.6), and in Bolivia ($69.7); but less than in Venezuela ($782.0), in Argentina ($366.5), and in Uruguay ($336.5). The growth of public expenditure in Brazil was greater than in Venezuela (2.1%), in Uruguay (1.5%), in Argentina (-0.17%), in Peru (-0.73%), and in Bolivia (-2.5%); but less than in Paraguay (5.6%) and in Colombia (5.1%).

Comparison with leaders. The public expenditure of Brazil was less than in the USA ($665.3 billion), in Japan ($257.4 billion), in Germany ($203.7 billion), in the USSR ($181.1 billion), and in France ($159.8 billion). The government expenditure per capita in Brazil was less than in France ($2.8 thousand), in the USA ($2.8 thousand), in Germany ($2.6 thousand), in Japan ($2.1 thousand), and in the USSR ($658.0). The growth of public expenditure in Brazil was greater than in France (2.8%), in the United States (2.6%), and in Germany (0.98%); but less than in the USSR (5.4%) and in Japan (3.5%).

The 1990s

The Brazil's government expenditure was $117.8 billion per year in the 1990s, ranked 8th in the world. The share in the world was 2.5%, and 7.7% in the Americas.

The share of government consumption expenditure in GDP of Brazil was 19.3% in the 1990s, ranked 65th in the world, and was on a par with Belarus (19.3%), Germany (19.3%), Estonia (19.4%).

The Brazil's public expenditure per capita was $733.0 in the 1990s, ranked 72nd in the world, and was on a par with Western Asia ($741.4), Saint Kitts and Nevis ($716.6). The government expenditure per capita in Brazil was less than government expenditure per capita in the world ($824.8) by 11.1%, and was less than public expenditure per capita in the Americas ($1 972.7) in 2.7 times.

The growth of government consumption expenditure in Brazil was -0.2% in the 1990s, ranked 154th in the world. The growth of public expenditure in Brazil (-0.22%) was less than growth of public expenditure in the world (2.0%), was less than growth of government consumption expenditure in the Americas (1.1%).

Comparison with neighbors. The Brazilian government expenditure was greater than in Argentina ($33.3 billion), in Colombia ($10.6 billion), in Venezuela ($10.2 billion), in Peru ($4.5 billion), in Uruguay ($2.1 billion), in Bolivia ($895.5 million), and in Paraguay ($797.4 million). The government expenditure per capita in Brazil was greater than in Uruguay ($653.6), in Venezuela ($468.9), in Colombia ($294.5), in Peru ($185.3), in Paraguay ($168.9), and in Bolivia ($118.6); but less than in Argentina ($962.8). The growth of government consumption expenditure in Brazil was greater than in Venezuela (-0.48%) and in Argentina (-0.58%); but less than in Colombia (9.9%), in Paraguay (4.0%), in Bolivia (3.2%), in Peru (3.2%), and in Uruguay (2.7%).

Comparison with leaders. The Brazilian government consumption expenditure was less than in the USA ($1.1 trillion), in Japan ($651.8 billion), in Germany ($419.6 billion), in France ($325.4 billion), and in the UK ($234.6 billion). The Brazil's government expenditure per capita was less than in France ($5.5 thousand), in Germany ($5.2 thousand), in Japan ($5.2 thousand), in the USA ($4.3 thousand), and in the UK ($4.1 thousand). The growth of government expenditure in Brazil was less than in Japan (3.0%), in Germany (2.4%), in the United Kingdom (2.1%), in France (1.8%), and in the USA (1.3%).

The 2000s

The government expenditure of Brazil was $185.4 billion per year in the 2000s, ranked 10th in the world. The share in the world was 2.4%, and 7.2% in the Americas.

The share of public expenditure in GDP of Brazil was 19.1% in the 2000s, ranked 53rd in the world, and was on a par with Croatia (19.1%), Southern Africa (19.0%), Latvia (19.0%).

The government expenditure per capita in Brazil was $1 003.2 in the 2000s, ranked 78th in the world, and was on a par with Eastern Europe ($993.3). The government expenditure per capita in Brazil was less than government expenditure per capita in the world ($1 200.9) by 16.5%, and was less than government expenditure per capita in the Americas ($2 931.6) in 2.9 times.

The growth of government expenditure in Brazil was 2.8% in the 2000s, ranked 130th in the world. The growth of government expenditure in Brazil (2.8%) was less than growth of government expenditure in the world (3.1%), was greater than growth of government expenditure in the Americas (2.4%).

Comparison with neighbors. The Brazil's public expenditure was greater than in Argentina ($32.6 billion), in Venezuela ($21.7 billion),

Chapter XII. Government consumption expenditure

in Colombia ($20.7 billion), in Peru ($8.8 billion), in Uruguay ($2.5 billion), in Bolivia ($1.6 billion), and in Paraguay ($1.1 billion). The public expenditure per capita in Brazil was greater than in Argentina ($842.9), in Venezuela ($830.1), in Uruguay ($741.0), in Colombia ($489.6), in Peru ($317.2), in Paraguay ($189.4), and in Bolivia ($178.2). The growth of public expenditure in Brazil was greater than in Paraguay (1.9%) and in Uruguay (1.2%); but less than in Venezuela (6.8%), in Peru (4.8%), in Colombia (3.4%), in Bolivia (3.3%), and in Argentina (2.9%).

Comparison with leaders. The government expenditure of Brazil was less than in the United States ($1.9 trillion), in Japan ($844.2 billion), in Germany ($520.1 billion), in France ($479.9 billion), and in the United Kingdom ($453.4 billion). The government expenditure per capita in Brazil was less than in France ($7.6 thousand), in the UK ($7.5 thousand), in Japan ($6.6 thousand), in the USA ($6.5 thousand), and in Germany ($6.4 thousand). The growth of government expenditure in Brazil was greater than in the United States (2.2%), in Japan (1.7%), in France (1.7%), and in Germany (1.4%); but less than in the United Kingdom (2.9%).

The 2010s

The government consumption expenditure of Brazil was $419.5 billion per year in the 2010s, ranked 7th in the world. The share in the world was 3.2%, and 10.7% in the Americas.

The share of public expenditure in GDP of Brazil was 19.4% in the 2010s, ranked 66th in the world, and was on a par with Italy (19.4%), San Marino (19.4%), Southern Europe (19.4%).

The Brazil's public expenditure per capita was $2 061.0 in the 2010s, ranked 80th in the world. The government consumption expenditure per capita in Brazil was greater than government expenditure per capita in the world ($1 785.1) by 15.5%, and was less than public expenditure per capita in the Americas ($4 034.3) by 48.9%.

The growth of public expenditure in Brazil was 0.9% in the 2010s, ranked 152nd in the world. The growth of public expenditure in Brazil (0.86%) was less than growth of public expenditure in the world (2.3%), was greater than growth of government expenditure in the Americas (0.45%).

Comparison with neighbors. The Brazil's government expenditure was 4.5 times higher than in Argentina ($92.5 billion), 8.8 times higher than in Colombia ($47.5 billion), 9.8 times higher than in Venezuela ($42.7 billion), 17.5 times higher than in Peru ($23.9 billion), 56.3 times higher than in Uruguay ($7.4 billion), 81.7 times higher than in Bolivia ($5.1 billion), and 105.2 times higher than in Paraguay ($4.0 billion). The government expenditure per capita in Brazil was 41.7% higher than in Venezuela ($1 454.7), 2.1 times higher than in Colombia ($999.5), 2.6 times higher than in Peru ($784.8), 3.4 times higher than in Paraguay ($599.8), and 4.3 times higher than in Bolivia ($475.8); but 5.6% lower than in Uruguay ($2.2 thousand) and 4.5% lower than in Argentina ($2.2 thousand). The growth of government consumption expenditure in Brazil was greater than in Venezuela (-8.2%); but less than in Peru (5.7%), in Bolivia (5.6%), in Colombia (5.2%), in Paraguay (4.7%), in Uruguay (2.6%), and in Argentina (2.5%).

Comparison with leaders. The Brazilian public expenditure was 6.3 times lower than in the United States ($2.7 trillion), 4.0 times lower than in China ($1.7 trillion), 2.5 times lower than in Japan ($1.0 trillion), 41.9% lower than in Germany ($721.6 billion), and 34.2% lower than in France ($637.9 billion). The public expenditure per capita in Brazil was 72.1% higher than in China ($1 197.3); but 4.7 times lower than in France ($9.6 thousand), 4.3 times lower than in Germany ($8.8 thousand), 4.0 times lower than in the USA ($8.3 thousand), and 4.0 times lower than in Japan ($8.2 thousand). The growth of government expenditure in Brazil was greater than in the United States (0.0052%); but less than in China (8.3%), in Germany (1.9%), in Japan (1.3%), and in France (1.3%).

Chapter XIII. Household consumption expenditure

(including Non-profit institutions serving households)

The Brazil's household expenditure rose from $71.1 billion per year in the 1970s to $1.4 trillion per year in the 2010s, that is by $1.3 trillion or 19.1 times. The change occurred at $1.1 trillion due to a 4.9-fold increase in prices, as also at $138.2 billion due to a 2.0-fold increase in per capita rate, as well as at $65.2 billion due to the rise in population. The average annual growth in household expenditure is 3.8%. The minimum value of household expenditure was in 1970 at $24.1 billion. The maximum value of household consumption expenditure was in 2011 at $1.6 trillion.

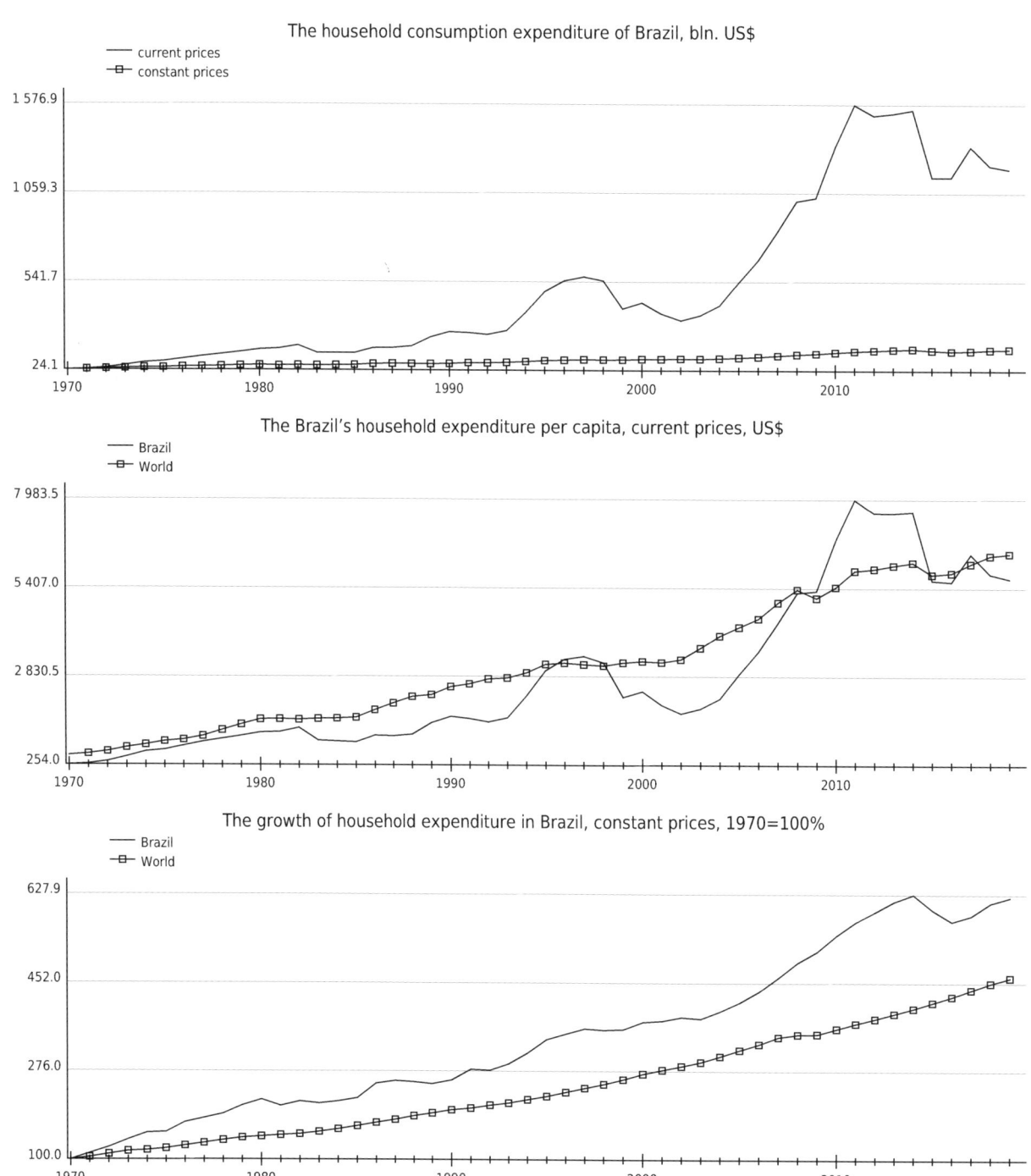

Chapter XIII. Household consumption expenditure

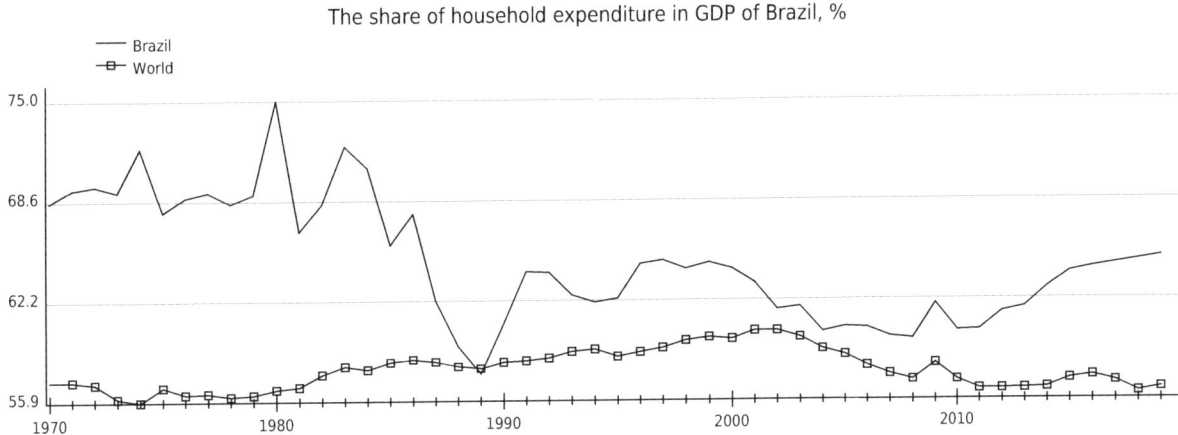
The share of household expenditure in GDP of Brazil, %

The 1970s

The household consumption expenditure of Brazil was $71.1 billion per year in the 1970s, ranked 11th in the world. The share in the world was 1.9%, and 5.1% in the Americas.

The share of household consumption expenditure in GDP of Brazil was 69.1% in the 1970s, ranked 73rd in the world, and was on a par with Kenya (69.2%), Uganda (69.4%), the British Virgin Islands (68.8%).

The household consumption expenditure per capita in Brazil was $669.4 in the 1970s, ranked 81st in the world, and was on a par with Colombia ($669.1), Iran ($682.6). The Brazilian household consumption expenditure per capita was less than household consumption expenditure per capita in the world ($914.8) by 26.8%, and was less than household expenditure per capita in the Americas ($2 467.5) in 3.7 times.

The growth of household consumption expenditure in Brazil was 8.5% in the 1970s, ranked 23rd in the world, and was on a par with Algeria (8.5%), Malta (8.5%). The growth of household consumption expenditure in Brazil (8.5%) was greater than growth of household expenditure in the world (4.1%), was greater than growth of household expenditure in the Americas (4.1%).

Comparison with neighbors. The household expenditure of Brazil was greater than in Argentina ($32.5 billion), in Colombia ($16.0 billion), in Venezuela ($11.0 billion), in Peru ($7.0 billion), in Uruguay ($2.9 billion), in Bolivia ($1.5 billion), and in Paraguay ($1.1 billion). The Brazilian household expenditure per capita was greater than in Colombia ($669.1), in Peru ($461.6), in Paraguay ($391.4), and in Bolivia ($298.8); but less than in Argentina ($1 267.5), in Uruguay ($1 030.4), and in Venezuela ($845.8). The growth of household consumption expenditure in Brazil was greater than in Venezuela (7.5%), in Paraguay (6.4%), in Colombia (5.7%), in Bolivia (3.4%), in Argentina (2.5%), in Peru (1.8%), and in Uruguay (1.1%).

Comparison with leaders. The household consumption expenditure of Brazil was less than in the USA ($1.0 trillion), in the USSR ($310.6 billion), in Japan ($280.9 billion), in Germany ($277.8 billion), and in France ($180.7 billion). The Brazil's household consumption expenditure per capita was less than in the USA ($4.7 thousand), in Germany ($3.5 thousand), in France ($3.4 thousand), in Japan ($2.5 thousand), and in the USSR ($1 231.6). The growth of household consumption expenditure in Brazil was greater than in Japan (5.1%), in the USSR (4.7%), in France (4.0%), in the United States (3.6%), and in Germany (3.6%).

The 1980s

The household consumption expenditure of Brazil was $151.8 billion per year in the 1980s, ranked 12th in the world. The share in the world was 1.7%, and 4.5% in the Americas.

The share of household expenditure in GDP of Brazil was 65.5% in the 1980s, ranked 89th in the world, and was on a par with the Philippines (65.5%), Namibia (65.4%), Central America (65.2%).

The Brazilian household expenditure per capita was $1 135.3 in the 1980s, ranked 89th in the world, and was on a par with Bulgaria ($1 132.3), Micronesia ($1 149.8), Ecuador ($1 159.3). The Brazil's household consumption expenditure per capita was less than household expenditure per capita in the world ($1 808.0) by 37.2%, and was less than household expenditure per capita in the Americas ($5 090.2) in 4.5 times.

The growth of household consumption expenditure in Brazil was 1.9% in the 1980s, ranked 131st in the world, and was on a par with Ghana (1.9%), Mexico (1.9%), Norway (1.9%). The growth of household expenditure in Brazil (1.9%) was less than growth of household consumption expenditure in the world (3.0%), was less than growth of household expenditure in the Americas (2.9%).

Comparison with neighbors. The Brazilian household expenditure was greater than in Argentina ($67.5 billion), in Colombia ($39.6 billion), in Venezuela ($28.3 billion), in Peru ($15.1 billion), in Uruguay ($5.7 billion), in Paraguay ($3.7 billion), and in Bolivia ($2.9 billion). The Brazil's household expenditure per capita was greater than in Paraguay ($1 014.8), in Peru ($769.5), and in Bolivia ($465.3); but less than in Argentina ($2.2 thousand), in Uruguay ($1 907.4), in Venezuela ($1 649.1), and in Colombia ($1 337.1). The growth of household consumption expenditure in Brazil was greater than in Venezuela (1.8%), in Uruguay (1.4%), in Bolivia (0.91%), in Peru (0.85%), and in Argentina (-0.19%); but less than in Paraguay (4.1%) and in Colombia (2.8%).

Comparison with leaders. The Brazilian household consumption expenditure was less than in the United States ($2.6 trillion), in Japan ($945.6 billion), in Germany ($575.7 billion), in the USSR ($424.6 billion), and in the United Kingdom ($416.5 billion). The Brazilian household expenditure per capita was less than in the United States ($10.9 thousand), in Japan ($7.8 thousand), in Germany ($7.4 thousand), in the United Kingdom ($7.4 thousand), and in the USSR ($1 542.8). The growth of household expenditure in Brazil was greater than in Germany (1.8%); but less than in Japan (3.7%), in the UK (3.5%), in the United States (3.2%), and in the USSR (3.0%).

The 1990s

The Brazilian household expenditure was $387.4 billion per year in the 1990s, ranked 7th in the world, and was on a par with Southern Asia ($394.8 billion). The share in the world was 2.3%, and 6.0% in the Americas.

The share of household consumption expenditure in GDP of Brazil was 63.6% in the 1990s, ranked 107th in the world, and was on a par with Chile (63.6%), Fiji (63.5%), Africa (63.9%).

The Brazil's household consumption expenditure per capita was $2 410.7 in the 1990s, ranked 73rd in the world, and was on a par with the Cook Islands ($2.4 thousand). The Brazil's household expenditure per capita was less than household consumption expenditure per capita in the world ($2 963.9) by 18.7%, and was less than household consumption expenditure per capita in the Americas ($8 394.4) in 3.5 times.

The growth of household expenditure in Brazil was 3.7% in the 1990s, ranked 74th in the world, and was on a par with South America (3.6%), Jamaica (3.6%), Brunei (3.6%). The growth of household expenditure in Brazil (3.7%) was greater than growth of household expenditure in the world (3.0%), was greater than growth of household expenditure in the Americas (3.3%).

Comparison with neighbors. The household expenditure of Brazil was greater than in Argentina ($190.6 billion), in Colombia ($67.7 billion), in Venezuela ($37.0 billion), in Peru ($32.8 billion), in Uruguay ($14.0 billion), in Paraguay ($6.4 billion), and in Bolivia ($5.1 billion). The Brazilian household expenditure per capita was greater than in Colombia ($1 877.5), in Venezuela ($1 705.7), in Paraguay ($1 363.0), in Peru ($1 360.2), and in Bolivia ($674.0); but less than in Argentina ($5.5 thousand) and in Uruguay ($4.4 thousand). The growth of household expenditure in Brazil was greater than in Bolivia (3.6%), in Peru (2.8%), in Colombia (2.0%), and in Venezuela (1.6%); but less than in Argentina (6.0%), in Paraguay (5.1%), and in Uruguay (4.6%).

Comparison with leaders. The household consumption expenditure of Brazil was less than in the United States ($4.9 trillion), in Japan ($2.3 trillion), in Germany ($1.2 trillion), in the United Kingdom ($884.5 billion), and in France ($783.0 billion). The Brazilian household consumption expenditure per capita was less than in the USA ($18.5 thousand), in Japan ($18.2 thousand), in the UK ($15.3 thousand), in Germany ($15.2 thousand), and in France ($13.2 thousand). The growth of household consumption expenditure in Brazil was greater than in the USA (3.4%), in the United Kingdom (2.8%), in Germany (2.1%), in Japan (1.8%), and in France (1.8%).

The 2000s

The household consumption expenditure of Brazil was $592.9 billion per year in the 2000s, ranked 10th in the world, and was on a par with Mexico ($592.0 billion), South-Eastern Asia ($582.4 billion). The share in the world was 2.2%, and 5.4% in the Americas.

The share of household consumption expenditure in GDP of Brazil was 61.0% in the 2000s, ranked 124th in the world, and was on a par with South Africa (61.1%), Syria (61.0%), Nigeria (60.9%).

The household consumption expenditure per capita in Brazil was $3 209.1 in the 2000s, ranked 87th in the world, and was on a par with Romania ($3.2 thousand), Jamaica ($3.1 thousand). The household consumption expenditure per capita in Brazil was less than household consumption expenditure per capita in the world ($4 208.2) by 23.7%, and was less than household expenditure per capita in the Americas ($12 522.4) in 3.9 times.

The growth of household expenditure in Brazil was 3.7% in the 2000s, ranked 115th in the world, and was on a par with Oceania

Chapter XIII. Household consumption expenditure

(3.6%), Trinidad and Tobago (3.6%), Bosnia and Herzegovina (3.7%). The growth of household consumption expenditure in Brazil (3.7%) was greater than growth of household expenditure in the world (3.0%), was greater than growth of household consumption expenditure in the Americas (2.7%).

Comparison with neighbors. The Brazil's household consumption expenditure was greater than in Argentina ($159.1 billion), in Colombia ($101.9 billion), in Venezuela ($92.1 billion), in Peru ($51.7 billion), in Uruguay ($14.6 billion), in Paraguay ($8.7 billion), and in Bolivia ($7.4 billion). The Brazilian household consumption expenditure per capita was greater than in Colombia ($2.4 thousand), in Peru ($1 865.7), in Paraguay ($1 515.7), and in Bolivia ($804.7); but less than in Uruguay ($4.4 thousand), in Argentina ($4.1 thousand), and in Venezuela ($3.5 thousand). The growth of household consumption expenditure in Brazil was greater than in Colombia (3.5%), in Bolivia (3.1%), in Paraguay (2.3%), in Argentina (2.3%), and in Uruguay (1.3%); but less than in Venezuela (6.3%) and in Peru (4.5%).

Comparison with leaders. The household expenditure of Brazil was less than in the USA ($8.5 trillion), in Japan ($2.6 trillion), in Germany ($1.5 trillion), in the United Kingdom ($1.5 trillion), and in France ($1.1 trillion). The Brazilian household expenditure per capita was less than in the United States ($28.8 thousand), in the United Kingdom ($25.0 thousand), in Japan ($20.4 thousand), in Germany ($18.9 thousand), and in France ($18.1 thousand). The growth of household expenditure in Brazil was greater than in the United States (2.4%), in the UK (2.1%), in France (2.0%), in Japan (0.81%), and in Germany (0.46%).

The 2010s

The Brazil's household expenditure was $1.4 trillion per year in the 2010s, ranked 7th in the world. The share in the world was 3.1%, and 8.0% in the Americas.

The share of household consumption expenditure in GDP of Brazil was 62.7% in the 2010s, ranked 118th in the world, and was on a par with the Bahamas (62.8%), Romania (62.8%), Vanuatu (62.5%).

The Brazilian household consumption expenditure per capita was $6 657.5 in the 2010s, ranked 79th in the world, and was on a par with Grenada ($6.6 thousand), Turkey ($6.6 thousand), Panama ($6.7 thousand). The Brazil's household consumption expenditure per capita was greater than household expenditure per capita in the world ($6 018.5) by 10.6%, and was less than household expenditure per capita in the Americas ($17 389.9) in 2.6 times.

The growth of household consumption expenditure in Brazil was 1.9% in the 2010s, ranked 147th in the world, and was on a par with the Cayman Islands (1.9%). The growth of household expenditure in Brazil (1.9%) was less than growth of household consumption expenditure in the world (2.8%), was less than growth of household expenditure in the Americas (2.2%).

Comparison with neighbors. The Brazilian household consumption expenditure was 3.8 times higher than in Argentina ($361.3 billion), 5.3 times higher than in Venezuela ($257.2 billion), 6.1 times higher than in Colombia ($220.9 billion), 10.9 times higher than in Peru ($124.4 billion), 37.9 times higher than in Uruguay ($35.8 billion), 58.0 times higher than in Paraguay ($23.4 billion), and 65.0 times higher than in Bolivia ($20.8 billion). The household consumption expenditure per capita in Brazil was 43.1% higher than in Colombia ($4.7 thousand), 63.3% higher than in Peru ($4.1 thousand), 89.3% higher than in Paraguay ($3.5 thousand), and 3.4 times higher than in Bolivia ($1 932.8); but 36.6% lower than in Uruguay ($10.5 thousand), 24.1% lower than in Venezuela ($8.8 thousand), and 21.0% lower than in Argentina ($8.4 thousand). The growth of household expenditure in Brazil was greater than in Argentina (1.8%) and in Venezuela (-9.1%); but less than in Peru (5.1%), in Bolivia (4.6%), in Paraguay (4.4%), in Colombia (3.9%), and in Uruguay (3.6%).

Comparison with leaders. The Brazilian household consumption expenditure was 9.0 times lower than in the USA ($12.2 trillion), 2.9 times lower than in China ($3.9 trillion), 2.2 times lower than in Japan ($3.0 trillion), 30.8% lower than in Germany ($2.0 trillion), and 24.0% lower than in the United Kingdom ($1.8 trillion). The Brazil's household expenditure per capita was 2.4 times higher than in China ($2.8 thousand); but 5.7 times lower than in the United States ($38.2 thousand), 4.1 times lower than in the UK ($27.2 thousand), 3.6 times lower than in Germany ($23.9 thousand), and 3.5 times lower than in Japan ($23.4 thousand). The growth of household expenditure in Brazil was greater than in the UK (1.8%), in Germany (1.4%), and in Japan (0.64%); but less than in China (8.3%) and in the United States (2.4%).

Chapter XIV. Food consumption

During the research period the food consumption grew in alcoholic beverages (in 4.1 times), meat (in 2.8 times), eggs (in 2.2 times), vegetable oils (in 2.1 times), milk (in 2.1 times), vegetables (by 94.7%), fish (by 44.4%), treenuts (by 38.0%), fruits (by 31.9%), stimulants (by 27.9%), spices (by 25.0%), cereals (by 11.7%), but fell in sugar (by 7.1%), pulses (by 20.0%), starchy roots (by 65.9%).

These are the correlation coefficients between the GNI per capita in constant prices and the food consumption: alcoholic beverages (0.997), milk (0.997), vegetables (0.996), meat (0.982), fruits (0.971), vegetable oils (0.94), eggs (0.916), cereals (0.813), stimulants (0.677), fish (0.667), treenuts (0.498), spices (0.422), pulses (-0.516), sugar (-0.621), starchy roots (-0.794).

The 1970s

Kcal supply in Brazil was 2 495.2 kcal/capita/day in the 1970s, ranked 59th in the world, and was on a par with Madagascar (2 514.2 kcal/capita/day), South America (2 514.6 kcal/capita/day), Paraguay (2 473.3 kcal/capita/day). Kcal supply in Brazil was greater than in the world (2 403.2 kcal/capita/day), and was less than in the Americas (2 754.7 kcal/capita/day). Structure of kcal supply: cereals (35.5%), sugar (17.8%), starchy roots (9%), vegetable oils (8.1%), pulses (7.3%), and others (22.3%).

Protein supply in Brazil was 60.8 g/capita/day in the 1970s, ranked 78th in the world, and was on a par with Melanesia (60.7 g/capita/day), Niger (61.0 g/capita/day), Uganda (60.2 g/capita/day). Protein supply in Brazil was less than in the world (65.0 g/capita/day), and was less than in the Americas (79.0 g/capita/day). Structure of protein supply: cereals (33%), pulses (19.6%), meat (18.2%), milk (10.3%), starchy roots (3.5%), and others (15.4%).

Fat supply in Brazil was 54.0 g/capita/day in the 1970s, ranked 72nd in the world, and was on a par with Ecuador (53.8 g/capita/day), Zimbabwe (53.6 g/capita/day), Albania (53.6 g/capita/day). Fat supply in Brazil was less than in the world (55.1 g/capita/day), and was less than in the Americas (85.8 g/capita/day). Structure of fat supply: vegetable oils (42.3%), meat (18.5%), milk (11.3%), cereals (4.3%), eggs (1.8%), and others (21.8%).

These are the levels of food consumption in the world rankings: 5th - pulses (19.7 kg/capita/yr), 20th - sugar (45.7 kg/capita/yr), 21st - stimulants (5.1 kg/capita/yr), 38th - starchy roots (100.0 kg/capita/yr), 44th - fruits (89.1 kg/capita/yr), 53rd - vegetable oils (8.3 kg/capita/yr), 57th - meat (32.9 kg/capita/yr), 65th - milk (71.6 kg/capita/yr), 67th - eggs (4.1 kg/capita/yr), 88th - alcoholic beverages (17.6 kg/capita/yr), 96th - fish (7.2 kg/capita/yr), 99th - vegetables (26.9 kg/capita/yr), 116th - spices (0.098 kg/capita/yr).

The 1980s

Kcal supply in Brazil was 2 656.4 kcal/capita/day in the 1980s, ranked 61st in the world, and was on a par with Polynesia (2 662.1 kcal/capita/day), Uruguay (2 665.2 kcal/capita/day), Cyprus (2 668.6 kcal/capita/day). Kcal supply in Brazil was greater than in the world (2 572.3 kcal/capita/day), and was less than in the Americas (2 917.7 kcal/capita/day). Structure of kcal supply: cereals (35.7%), sugar (17.8%), vegetable oils (11.8%), meat (6.5%), starchy roots (6.2%), and others (22%).

Protein supply in Brazil was 64.1 g/capita/day in the 1980s, ranked 81st in the world, and was on a par with Dominica (64.1 g/capita/day), Eastern Asia (64.2 g/capita/day), Botswana (64.4 g/capita/day). Protein supply in Brazil was less than in the world (69.1 g/capita/day), and was less than in the Americas (81.7 g/capita/day). Structure of protein supply: cereals (33.9%), meat (22%), pulses (14.8%), milk (11.6%), eggs (2.8%), and others (14.9%).

Fat supply in Brazil was 68.3 g/capita/day in the 1980s, ranked 66th in the world, and was on a par with Mauritius (68.3 g/capita/day), Dominica (68.6 g/capita/day), Paraguay (68.8 g/capita/day). Fat supply in Brazil was greater than in the world (63.2 g/capita/day), and was less than in the Americas (96.3 g/capita/day). Structure of fat supply: vegetable oils (51.7%), meat (18.3%), milk (10.4%), cereals (3.7%), eggs (2.3%), and others (13.6%).

These are the levels of food consumption in the world rankings: 6th - pulses (15.7 kg/capita/yr), 16th - sugar (48.6 kg/capita/yr), 33rd - vegetable oils (12.9 kg/capita/yr), 36th - stimulants (4.1 kg/capita/yr), 44th - fruits (89.1 kg/capita/yr), 51st - eggs (6.5 kg/capita/yr), 53rd - starchy roots (72.5 kg/capita/yr), 55th - meat (41.5 kg/capita/yr), 62nd - milk (84.5 kg/capita/yr), 71st - alcoholic beverages (27.1 kg/capita/yr), 82nd - treenuts (0.31 kg/capita/yr), 92nd - cereals (111.5 kg/capita/yr), 97th - vegetables (31.5 kg/capita/yr), 108th - fish (6.5 kg/capita/yr), 114th - spices (0.13 kg/capita/yr).

The 1990s

Kcal supply in Brazil was 2 808.3 kcal/capita/day in the 1990s, ranked 59th in the world, and was on a par with French Polynesia (2

Chapter XIV. Food consumption

811.6 kcal/capita/day), Central America (2 813.0 kcal/capita/day), South Africa (2 820.9 kcal/capita/day). Kcal supply in Brazil was greater than in the world (2 652.6 kcal/capita/day), and was less than in the Americas (3 035.8 kcal/capita/day). Structure of kcal supply: cereals (32.1%), sugar (17.1%), vegetable oils (12.2%), meat (9.9%), milk (6.2%), and others (22.5%).

Protein supply in Brazil was 73.0 g/capita/day in the 1990s, ranked 76th in the world, and was on a par with China (72.9 g/capita/day), Malaysia (72.7 g/capita/day), South Africa (73.4 g/capita/day). Protein supply in Brazil was greater than in the world (72.1 g/capita/day), and was less than in the Americas (86.2 g/capita/day). Structure of protein supply: meat (29.2%), cereals (28.3%), pulses (13.2%), milk (12.6%), eggs (2.8%), and others (13.9%).

Fat supply in Brazil was 83.3 g/capita/day in the 1990s, ranked 55th in the world, and was on a par with the Bahamas (83.8 g/capita/day). Fat supply in Brazil was greater than in the world (69.0 g/capita/day), and was less than in the Americas (100.9 g/capita/day). Structure of fat supply: vegetable oils (46.7%), meat (25.1%), milk (11%), cereals (2.9%), eggs (2.1%), and others (12.2%).

These are the levels of food consumption in the world rankings: 4th - pulses (16.0 kg/capita/yr), 13th - sugar (49.2 kg/capita/yr), 36th - vegetable oils (14.2 kg/capita/yr), 39th - fruits (101.6 kg/capita/yr), 45th - meat (63.1 kg/capita/yr), 49th - stimulants (3.8 kg/capita/yr), 57th - eggs (7.4 kg/capita/yr), 61st - alcoholic beverages (40.7 kg/capita/yr), 67th - milk (104.5 kg/capita/yr), 75th - starchy roots (61.3 kg/capita/yr), 106th - treenuts (0.37 kg/capita/yr), 118th - fish (5.8 kg/capita/yr), 119th - vegetables (36.2 kg/capita/yr), 120th - cereals (105.9 kg/capita/yr), 131st - spices (0.14 kg/capita/yr).

The 2000s

Kcal supply in Brazil was 3 047.2 kcal/capita/day in the 2000s, ranked 48th in the world, and was on a par with Western Asia (3 042.3 kcal/capita/day), Iran (3 040.8 kcal/capita/day), Northern Africa (3 054.7 kcal/capita/day). Kcal supply in Brazil was greater than in the world (2 765.9 kcal/capita/day), and was less than in the Americas (3 186.4 kcal/capita/day). Structure of kcal supply: cereals (31%), vegetable oils (13.4%), sugar (13.2%), meat (12%), milk (6.6%), and others (23.8%).

Protein supply in Brazil was 83.9 g/capita/day in the 2000s, ranked 64th in the world, and was on a par with Macao (83.9 g/capita/day), Kyrgyzstan (84.0 g/capita/day), Mauritius (83.7 g/capita/day). Protein supply in Brazil was greater than in the world (76.5 g/capita/day), and was less than in the Americas (91.2 g/capita/day). Structure of protein supply: meat (32.1%), cereals (26.1%), milk (12.6%), pulses (11.9%), eggs (2.4%), and others (14.9%).

Fat supply in Brazil was 104.5 g/capita/day in the 2000s, ranked 43rd in the world, and was on a par with Turkey (104.6 g/capita/day). Fat supply in Brazil was greater than in the world (76.9 g/capita/day), and was less than in the Americas (113.5 g/capita/day). Structure of fat supply: vegetable oils (44.1%), meat (26.8%), milk (10.3%), cereals (2.6%), eggs (1.7%), and others (14.5%).

These are the levels of food consumption in the world rankings: 7th - pulses (16.5 kg/capita/yr), 25th - vegetable oils (16.8 kg/capita/yr), 32nd - meat (79.9 kg/capita/yr), 38th - stimulants (6.4 kg/capita/yr), 45th - sugar (41.3 kg/capita/yr), 48th - fruits (105.8 kg/capita/yr), 56th - alcoholic beverages (54.9 kg/capita/yr), 66th - eggs (7.4 kg/capita/yr), 67th - milk (119.9 kg/capita/yr), 75th - starchy roots (61.6 kg/capita/yr), 121st - fish (6.6 kg/capita/yr), 122nd - cereals (111.8 kg/capita/yr), 123rd - vegetables (44.7 kg/capita/yr), 128th - treenuts (0.34 kg/capita/yr), 134th - spices (0.19 kg/capita/yr).

The 2010s

Kcal supply in Brazil was 3 256.8 kcal/capita/day in the 2010s, ranked 35th in the world, and was on a par with Czechia (3 256.5 kcal/capita/day), Australia (3 245.8 kcal/capita/day), Estonia (3 271.0 kcal/capita/day). Kcal supply in Brazil was greater than in the world (2 869.3 kcal/capita/day), and was greater than in the Americas (3 219.3 kcal/capita/day). Structure of kcal supply: cereals (29.4%), vegetable oils (13.2%), meat (13.2%), sugar (12.8%), milk (7.7%), and others (23.7%).

Protein supply in Brazil was 93.7 g/capita/day in the 2010s, ranked 49th in the world, and was on a par with New Zealand (93.7 g/capita/day), Switzerland (93.9 g/capita/day), Latvia (94.1 g/capita/day). Protein supply in Brazil was greater than in the world (80.6 g/capita/day), and was greater than in the Americas (92.7 g/capita/day). Structure of protein supply: meat (33.6%), cereals (23.9%), milk (14%), pulses (10.6%), fish (2.9%), and others (15%).

Fat supply in Brazil was 115.8 g/capita/day in the 2010s, ranked 42nd in the world, and was on a par with Malta (115.8 g/capita/day), Kuwait (116.1 g/capita/day). Fat supply in Brazil was greater than in the world (82.4 g/capita/day), and was less than in the Americas (118.2 g/capita/day). Structure of fat supply: vegetable oils (41.8%), meat (28.3%), milk (11.5%), cereals (2.4%), eggs (1.9%), and others (14.1%).

These are the levels of food consumption in the world rankings: 11th - pulses (16.4 kg/capita/yr), 16th - meat (93.4 kg/capita/yr), 29th - vegetable oils (17.7 kg/capita/yr), 37th - fruits (117.6 kg/capita/yr), 43rd - stimulants (6.5 kg/capita/yr), 45th - alcoholic beverages (72.1 kg/capita/yr), 53rd - milk (148.5 kg/capita/yr), 61st - eggs (8.8 kg/capita/yr), 70th - starchy roots (60.3 kg/capita/yr), 105th - fish (10.3 kg/capita/yr), 112th - treenuts (0.71 kg/capita/yr), 114th - vegetables (52.3 kg/capita/yr), 121st - cereals (114.9 kg/capita/yr), 146th - spices (0.12 kg/capita/yr).

Part V. Reproduction

Chapter XV. Gross fixed capital formation

(including Acquisitions less disposals of valuables)

The Brazilian gross fixed capital formation rose from $22.6 billion per year in the 1970s to $398.0 billion per year in the 2010s, that is by $375.4 billion or 17.6 times. The change occurred at $342.8 billion due to a 7.2-fold increase in prices, as also at $11.9 billion due to a 1.3-fold increase in per capita rate, as well as at $20.7 billion due to the growth in population. The average annual growth in fixed capital formation is 2.8%. The minimum value of fixed capital formation was in 1970 at $6.6 billion. The maximum value of fixed capital formation was in 2011 at $539.2 billion.

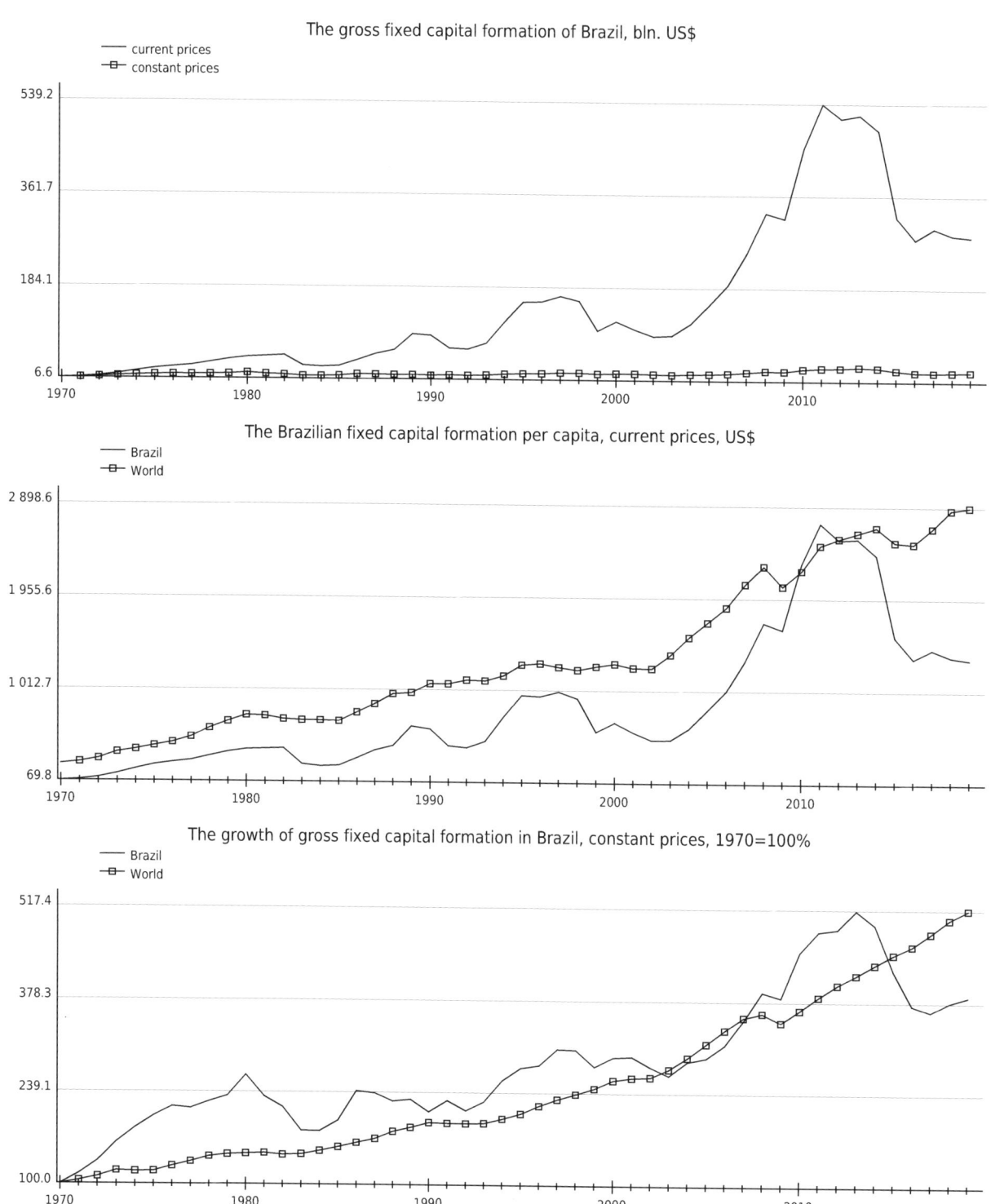

Chapter XV. Gross fixed capital formation

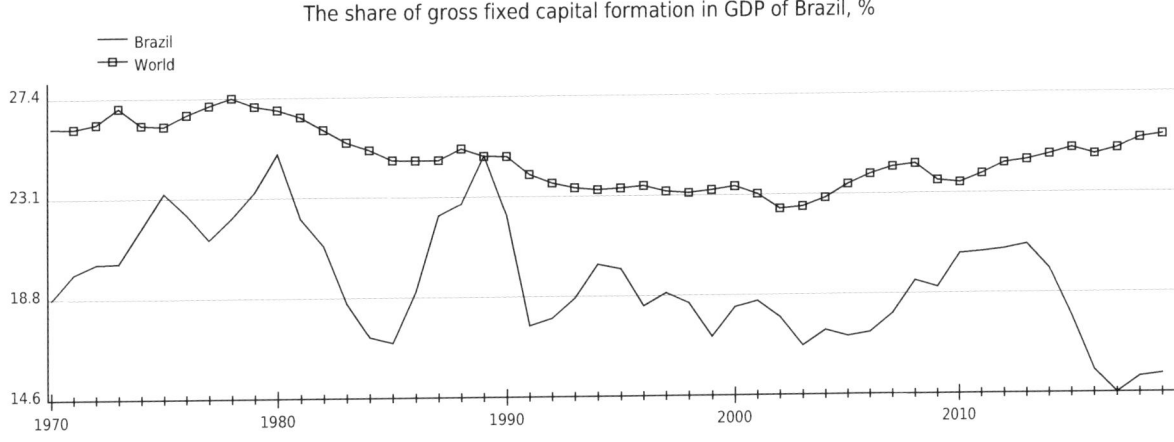

The share of gross fixed capital formation in GDP of Brazil, %

The 1970s

The Brazil's fixed capital formation was $22.6 billion per year in the 1970s, ranked 14th in the world, and was on a par with Central America ($22.7 billion), the Netherlands ($23.1 billion). The share in the world was 1.3%, and 4.4% in the Americas.

The share of gross fixed capital formation in GDP of Brazil was 22.0% in the 1970s, ranked 105th in the world, and was on a par with the Solomon Islands (21.9%), Saudi Arabia (22.1%), the Caribbean (22.1%).

The Brazilian fixed capital formation per capita was $212.9 in the 1970s, ranked 91st in the world, and was on a par with Congo ($212.1), the Federated States of Micronesia ($210.9). The gross fixed capital formation per capita in Brazil was less than fixed capital formation per capita in the world ($433.5) in 2.0 times, and was less than fixed capital formation per capita in the Americas ($913.4) in 4.3 times.

The growth of gross fixed capital formation in Brazil was 9.9% in the 1970s, ranked 44th in the world. The growth of gross fixed capital formation in Brazil (9.9%) was greater than growth of gross fixed capital formation in the world (4.2%), was greater than growth of fixed capital formation in the Americas (5.3%).

Comparison with neighbors. The Brazil's gross fixed capital formation was greater than in Venezuela ($14.6 billion), in Argentina ($11.1 billion), in Colombia ($4.7 billion), in Peru ($1.8 billion), in Uruguay ($763.9 million), in Paraguay ($511.7 million), and in Bolivia ($393.4 million). The gross fixed capital formation per capita in Brazil was greater than in Colombia ($198.2), in Paraguay ($184.8), in Peru ($117.8), and in Bolivia ($79.4); but less than in Venezuela ($1 117.3), in Argentina ($434.4), and in Uruguay ($269.0). The growth of gross fixed capital formation in Brazil was greater than in Uruguay (8.4%), in Bolivia (6.8%), in Peru (6.3%), in Colombia (4.3%), and in Argentina (3.1%); but less than in Paraguay (17.3%) and in Venezuela (10.1%).

Comparison with leaders. The Brazilian gross fixed capital formation was less than in the United States ($381.9 billion), in the USSR ($214.6 billion), in Japan ($191.6 billion), in Germany ($125.8 billion), and in France ($82.9 billion). The fixed capital formation per capita in Brazil was less than in the USA ($1 750.0), in Japan ($1 720.7), in Germany ($1 597.2), in France ($1 545.4), and in the USSR ($850.9). The growth of fixed capital formation in Brazil was greater than in the United States (4.4%), in Japan (3.9%), in the USSR (3.2%), in France (2.7%), and in Germany (1.5%).

The 1980s

The gross fixed capital formation of Brazil was $49.7 billion per year in the 1980s, ranked 14th in the world, and was on a par with Central America ($49.5 billion). The share in the world was 1.3%, and 4.1% in the Americas.

The share of fixed capital formation in GDP of Brazil was 21.4% in the 1980s, ranked 103rd in the world, and was on a par with Indonesia (21.4%), Macao (21.5%), the Dominican Republic (21.5%).

The Brazil's fixed capital formation per capita was $371.8 in the 1980s, ranked 95th in the world, and was on a par with Dominica ($376.5). The gross fixed capital formation per capita in Brazil was less than fixed capital formation per capita in the world ($790.9) in 2.1 times, and was less than gross fixed capital formation per capita in the Americas ($1 848.1) in 5.0 times.

The growth of fixed capital formation in Brazil was -0.2% in the 1980s, ranked 128th in the world. The growth of fixed capital formation in Brazil (-0.19%) was less than growth of fixed capital formation in the world (2.5%), was less than growth of gross fixed capital formation in the Americas (1.9%).

Comparison with neighbors. The Brazil's fixed capital formation was greater than in Venezuela ($19.2 billion), in Argentina ($16.3 billion), in Colombia ($13.5 billion), in Peru ($4.8 billion), in Paraguay ($1.8 billion), in Uruguay ($1.3 billion), and in Bolivia ($506.6 million). The Brazil's fixed capital formation per capita was greater than in Peru ($245.8) and in Bolivia ($82.6); but less than in Venezuela ($1 120.0), in Argentina ($544.0), in Paraguay ($500.3), in Colombia ($456.7), and in Uruguay ($436.2). The growth of fixed capital formation in Brazil was greater than in Peru (-1.1%), in Bolivia (-4.0%), in Argentina (-5.6%), in Uruguay (-5.9%), and in Venezuela (-7.1%); but less than in Colombia (3.2%) and in Paraguay (2.1%).

Comparison with leaders. The fixed capital formation of Brazil was less than in the United States ($958.4 billion), in Japan ($571.7 billion), in the USSR ($271.0 billion), in Germany ($238.1 billion), and in France ($164.3 billion). The Brazilian fixed capital formation per capita was less than in Japan ($4.7 thousand), in the United States ($4.0 thousand), in Germany ($3.1 thousand), in France ($2.9 thousand), and in the USSR ($984.8). The growth of gross fixed capital formation in Brazil was less than in Japan (4.8%), in the United States (3.1%), in France (2.4%), in the USSR (1.7%), and in Germany (1.4%).

The 1990s

The Brazil's fixed capital formation was $115.5 billion per year in the 1990s, ranked 11th in the world. The share in the world was 1.7%, and 5.6% in the Americas.

The share of gross fixed capital formation in GDP of Brazil was 19.0% in the 1990s, ranked 147th in the world, and was on a par with Georgia (19.0%), Guatemala (19.0%), the UK (18.8%).

The fixed capital formation per capita in Brazil was $718.4 in the 1990s, ranked 85th in the world, and was on a par with South America ($722.0). The Brazilian fixed capital formation per capita was less than fixed capital formation per capita in the world ($1 183.8) by 39.3%, and was less than fixed capital formation per capita in the Americas ($2 694.1) in 3.8 times.

The growth of fixed capital formation in Brazil was 2% in the 1990s, ranked 125th in the world, and was on a par with the Federated States of Micronesia (2.0%). The growth of gross fixed capital formation in Brazil (2.0%) was less than growth of fixed capital formation in the world (2.8%), was less than growth of gross fixed capital formation in the Americas (4.4%).

Comparison with neighbors. The gross fixed capital formation of Brazil was greater than in Argentina ($40.0 billion), in Colombia ($21.9 billion), in Venezuela ($17.1 billion), in Peru ($9.5 billion), in Uruguay ($2.9 billion), in Paraguay ($2.4 billion), and in Bolivia ($1.1 billion). The gross fixed capital formation per capita in Brazil was greater than in Colombia ($608.1), in Paraguay ($510.7), in Peru ($395.0), and in Bolivia ($151.6); but less than in Argentina ($1 156.9), in Uruguay ($903.3), and in Venezuela ($788.0). The growth of fixed capital formation in Brazil was greater than in Paraguay (-1.2%) and in Colombia (-1.2%); but less than in Bolivia (9.7%), in Argentina (7.4%), in Uruguay (7.2%), in Peru (6.0%), and in Venezuela (2.9%).

Comparison with leaders. The fixed capital formation of Brazil was less than in the USA ($1.6 trillion), in Japan ($1.3 trillion), in Germany ($520.7 billion), in France ($299.3 billion), and in the UK ($250.0 billion). The Brazil's gross fixed capital formation per capita was less than in Japan ($10.4 thousand), in Germany ($6.5 thousand), in the United States ($6.1 thousand), in France ($5.0 thousand), and in the United Kingdom ($4.3 thousand). The growth of gross fixed capital formation in Brazil was greater than in the United Kingdom (1.7%), in France (1.5%), and in Japan (0.18%); but less than in the United States (4.8%) and in Germany (2.4%).

The 2000s

The Brazil's fixed capital formation was $176.6 billion per year in the 2000s, ranked 14th in the world, and was on a par with Russia ($172.9 billion). The share in the world was 1.6%, and 4.9% in the Americas.

The share of fixed capital formation in GDP of Brazil was 18.2% in the 2000s, ranked 172nd in the world, and was on a par with Tajikistan (18.3%), Barbados (18.1%), Dominica (18.3%).

The Brazil's gross fixed capital formation per capita was $955.7 in the 2000s, ranked 101st in the world, and was on a par with Belarus ($955.6), South America ($932.4). The gross fixed capital formation per capita in Brazil was less than fixed capital formation per capita in the world ($1 690.7) by 43.5%, and was less than gross fixed capital formation per capita in the Americas ($4 079.3) in 4.3 times.

The growth of fixed capital formation in Brazil was 3.3% in the 2000s, ranked 124th in the world, and was on a par with Micronesia (3.3%). The growth of fixed capital formation in Brazil (3.3%) was less than growth of gross fixed capital formation in the world (3.5%), was greater than growth of fixed capital formation in the Americas (1.3%).

Comparison with neighbors. The Brazilian fixed capital formation was greater than in Argentina ($38.7 billion), in Venezuela ($38.4

Chapter XV. Gross fixed capital formation

billion), in Colombia ($31.2 billion), in Peru ($15.4 billion), in Uruguay ($3.4 billion), in Paraguay ($2.5 billion), and in Bolivia ($1.7 billion). The gross fixed capital formation per capita in Brazil was greater than in Colombia ($738.3), in Peru ($556.0), in Paraguay ($440.8), and in Bolivia ($182.0); but less than in Venezuela ($1 465.6), in Uruguay ($1 028.9), and in Argentina ($1 000.0). The growth of fixed capital formation in Brazil was greater than in Uruguay (2.5%), in Argentina (2.2%), and in Bolivia (1.8%); but less than in Colombia (9.3%), in Peru (7.1%), in Venezuela (6.6%), and in Paraguay (3.5%).

Comparison with leaders. The Brazil's fixed capital formation was less than in the United States ($2.8 trillion), in Japan ($1.2 trillion), in China ($1.0 trillion), in Germany ($557.7 billion), and in France ($463.9 billion). The Brazilian fixed capital formation per capita was greater than in China ($782.2); but less than in the USA ($9.4 thousand), in Japan ($9.0 thousand), in France ($7.4 thousand), and in Germany ($6.9 thousand). The growth of fixed capital formation in Brazil was greater than in France (1.6%), in the USA (0.43%), in Germany (-0.56%), and in Japan (-2.0%); but less than in China (13.4%).

The 2010s

The gross fixed capital formation of Brazil was $398.0 billion per year in the 2010s, ranked 10th in the world, and was on a par with Canada ($400.6 billion), Australasia ($404.2 billion). The share in the world was 2.1%, and 7.7% in the Americas.

The share of gross fixed capital formation in GDP of Brazil was 18.4% in the 2010s, ranked 166th in the world, and was on a par with Belize (18.5%), Polynesia (18.3%), Costa Rica (18.5%).

The fixed capital formation per capita in Brazil was $1 955.6 in the 2010s, ranked 93rd in the world, and was on a par with Mauritius ($1 955.2), the Cook Islands ($1 937.5), Costa Rica ($1 994.2). The fixed capital formation per capita in Brazil was less than gross fixed capital formation per capita in the world ($2 621.1) by 25.4%, and was less than fixed capital formation per capita in the Americas ($5 284.2) in 2.7 times.

The growth of gross fixed capital formation in Brazil was 0.1% in the 2010s, ranked 169th in the world. The growth of fixed capital formation in Brazil (0.067%) was less than growth of fixed capital formation in the world (4.1%), was less than growth of gross fixed capital formation in the Americas (2.9%).

Comparison with neighbors. The Brazil's gross fixed capital formation was 4.7 times higher than in Argentina ($85.6 billion), 5.5 times higher than in Venezuela ($73.0 billion), 5.5 times higher than in Colombia ($72.3 billion), 8.9 times higher than in Peru ($44.6 billion), 38.7 times higher than in Uruguay ($10.3 billion), 55.1 times higher than in Paraguay ($7.2 billion), and 62.7 times higher than in Bolivia ($6.3 billion). The fixed capital formation per capita in Brazil was 28.5% higher than in Colombia ($1 522.0), 33.6% higher than in Peru ($1 463.4), 79.9% higher than in Paraguay ($1 086.9), and 3.3 times higher than in Bolivia ($588.5); but 35.2% lower than in Uruguay ($3.0 thousand), 21.4% lower than in Venezuela ($2.5 thousand), and 2.1% lower than in Argentina ($1 997.2). The growth of gross fixed capital formation in Brazil was greater than in Venezuela (-19.5%); but less than in Bolivia (7.3%), in Colombia (4.7%), in Paraguay (4.4%), in Peru (4.4%), in Uruguay (1.5%), and in Argentina (1.3%).

Comparison with leaders. The fixed capital formation of Brazil was 11.4 times lower than in China ($4.5 trillion), 9.0 times lower than in the USA ($3.6 trillion), 3.0 times lower than in Japan ($1.2 trillion), 47.1% lower than in Germany ($752.5 billion), and 42.9% lower than in India ($696.8 billion). The gross fixed capital formation per capita in Brazil was 3.7 times higher than in India ($535.2); but 5.8 times lower than in the United States ($11.3 thousand), 4.8 times lower than in Japan ($9.5 thousand), 4.7 times lower than in Germany ($9.2 thousand), and 39.4% lower than in China ($3.2 thousand). The growth of gross fixed capital formation in Brazil was less than in China (8.0%), in India (5.8%), in the USA (3.8%), in Germany (2.8%), and in Japan (1.8%).

Made in the USA
Middletown, DE
05 October 2021